The Boxer

Handbook

Joan Hustace Walker

With Full-color Photographs

BARRON'S

Acknowledgments

This book could not have been written without the tremendous support and tireless help of many Boxer fanciers in both Germany and the United States. I would like to express my deepest appreciation to German Boxer fanciers Rosi Westphal, Willibald Wendel, and the Rausch family, Heinrich Mörtl, the many enthusiastic members of the Wetzlar, Germany training club, and the Boxer Klub e.v. Sitz München. Among the American Boxer fanciers, I would like to extend a special thank you to Tracy Hendrickson, Wendy Wallner, D.V.M., Calvin Gruver, Cathy Markos, Ann Gilbert, Molly Bachman, and Mary Stocker. And, of course, my gratitude to my husband, Randy, and my children, Eric and Grace, for their unwavering support during the researching and writing of this book, and for their mutual love of dogs.

Cover Credits

Front and back: Tracy Hendrickson, Billy Hustace, Curtis Hustace; inside front and back: Tracy Hendrickson

All inquiries should be addressed to:
Barron's Educational Series, Inc.
250 Wireless Boulevard
Hauppauge, New York 11788
http://www.barronseduc.com

ISBN-13: 978-0-7641-1244-7
ISBN-10: 0-7641-1244-9

Library of Congress Catalog Card No. 99-55898

Library of Congress Cataloging-in-Publication Data
Walker, Joan Hustace, 1962–
    The boxer handbook / Joan Hustace Walker.
    p. cm.
    Includes bibliographical references (p.   ).
    ISBN 0-7641-1244-9
    1. Boxer (Dog breed). I. Title.
SF429.B75 W36   2000
639.73—dc21
                        99-55898
                        CIP

Printed in China

13 12

About the Author

Joan Hustace Walker has been writing professionally since 1984. She is a member of the Authors Guild, the American Society of Journalists and Authors, the Dog Writers Association of America, the Cat Writers Association, and the Society of Environmental Journalists. Walker writes for both general and technical audiences, specializing in animals, education, aging, and environmental issues. Her other book titles include *St. Bernards, Old English Sheepdogs,* and *Great Pyrenees.* She has had more than 100 articles published by a variety of magazines, including *Modern Maturity, Family Circle,* and *Dog World* and was awarded the "Maxwell Award" by the Dog Writers Association.

Photo Credits

Tracy Hendrickson: pages 12, 17, 21, 24, 28, 29, 48, 51, 73, 86, 89, 94, 97, 98, 100, 102, 103, 104, 107, 108, 112, 153, 172, 174, 178, 185, 191; Billy Hustace: pages 25–27, 41, 46, 55, 63–65, 79, 80, 82, 115, 119, 121, 123, 124, 127, 129, 130, 144, 156, 170, 176, 180, 181, 184, 198; Curtis Hustace: pages 2, 4, 5, 8, 11, 13, 14, 16, 18, 20, 32, 34, 42, 44, 57, 60, 62, 71, 72, 74, 76, 78, 85, 88, 91, 95, 113, 114, 133, 134, 137, 140, 142, 146, 148, 149, 151, 160–164, 166, 167, 188, 190; Jean Wentworth: pages 36, 38, 47, 52.

Important Note

This pet handbook gives advice to the reader about buying and caring for a new dog. The author and publisher consider it important to point out that the advice given in the book applies to normally developed puppies or adult dogs, obtained from recognized dog breeders or adoption shelters, dogs that have been examined and are in excellent health with good temperament.

Anyone who adopts a grown dog should be aware that the animal has already formed its basic knowledge of human beings and their customs. The new owner should watch the animal carefully, especially its attitude and behavior toward humans. If possible, the new owner should meet the former owners before adopting the dog. If the dog is adopted from a shelter, the new owner should make an effort to obtain information about the dog's background, personality, and peculiarities. Dogs that come from abusive homes or from homes in which they have been treated abnormally may react to handling in an unnatural manner, and may have a tendency to snap or bite. Dogs with this nature should only be adopted by people who have had experience with such dogs.

Caution is further advised in the association of children with dogs, both puppies and adults, and in meeting other dogs, whether on or off lead.

Well-behaved and carefully supervised dogs may cause damage to someone else's property or cause accidents. It is therefore in the owner's interest to be adequately insured against such eventualities, and we strongly urge all dog owners to purchase a liability policy that covers their dog.

Contents

Preface

The Boxer Handbook was never meant to be kept on a shelf. This book is, and will be, an ongoing resource of information for past, present, and future fanciers of the breed. The book's vast amount of detailed information will enhance your enjoyment and care of one of the world's most admired breeds. It will be your guide from beginning to end—from finding the perfect puppy and raising him through his formative years, to enjoying middle age, and finally, saying good-bye at the end of his life.

In addition to noting the content of the book, it is worthwhile to footnote the extensive research, work, and writing that went into developing this book. The author, Joan Hustace Walker, is an acclaimed dog writer and is recognized for her high journalistic standards. In researching the Boxer's history for *The Boxer Handbook,* Walker traveled to the breed's origins in Germany, visited the German Boxer Klub in Munich, attended club training sessions, and interviewed numerous respected breed wardens, noted breeders, and German Boxer owners. She also translated German history and breed information, imparting some historical information to this book that has never before been published in the United States. For current Boxer information, she consulted with a variety of experts in the Boxer world, assuring that sensitive issues such as ear cropping, white Boxers, and major health issues were covered with depth and accuracy. Walker's meticulous research and her enthusiasm and understanding of the breed shine through on every page.

Most importantly, *The Boxer Handbook* has successfully captured the essence of the Boxer, which is truly a "mixed" breed in the sense that its character is part Boxer and part human. *The Boxer Handbook* brings the endearing, devoted, and comical characteristics of the breed to the surface for everyone to enjoy and understand. I hope you, too, will enjoy *The Boxer Handbook* and find this book a great reference.

For the Breed in Need,
Tracy L. Hendrickson
Founder and President of
The American Boxer Rescue
Association

Chapter One

History of the Boxer

The Boxer originated in southern Germany more than 100 years ago. Today, the Boxer has become one of the best loved and most popular breeds, not only in its homeland, but in many other areas of the world, as well. And for good reason. In addition to cutting a striking image with its well-muscled physique, classic, chiseled head, and smooth, glossy coat, the Boxer is extremely versatile.

Boxers are wonderful family dogs as well as keen competitors in both show and performance events. The Boxer is just as comfortable playing endless games of catch (or catch me!) with the kids in the backyard as it is striking a pose in the show ring or flying through suspended tires in agility competitions. Many Boxers still have what it takes to be superlative Schutzhund dogs—tracking, obedience, and protection work— and continue to be used today in drug detection, search and rescue, and even police work. But above all, the Boxer is a loyal and loving companion that truly lives to please its owner.

Early History

The friendly, congenial Boxer of today has its origins in a now-extinct hunting breed that dates back to the Middle Ages, the Brabanter Bullenbeisser. This strong, agile dog is said to have originated in Brabant, Belgium, and was used by noblemen to hunt wild boars in southern Germany. To the north and in Poland, a much larger bull-baiting dog was being used, called the Danziger Bullenbeisser. Historical accounts of the Brabanter Bullenbeisser note that the dog was dark in color, usually fawn or brindle with a black mask. The dog also had an undershot jaw so that it could hold onto the boar and still breathe through its nose. It is said that the Brabanter Bullenbeisser tackled game from the back and grabbed the animal by its neck or back, similarly to the manner in which Boxers were originally trained in early protection work. The ears of the Brabanter Bullenbeisser were cropped closely in order to prevent the boar from ripping an ear, a potentially bloody and serious injury.

The Boxer is a popular and versatile breed.

After the Napoleonic wars, the aristocracy who owned packs of Brabanter Bullenbeissers were dispersed. The talented dog, however, quickly found a new job as the local butcher or cattle dealer's dog. In this position, the smaller Bullenbeisser was used to hold and help control an animal for the butcher or cattle dealer. By the 1800s the Bullenbeisser was no longer a dog of the elite, but was now a dog of the working class. When not at work, the breed was a family pet and guardian of the home, captivating an increasing number of Germans.

It is thought that around 1830 an early form of the English Bulldog, one that was much taller and with a much smaller head than today's show dogs, was interbred with the Brabanter Bullenbeisser. This crossing makes sense, since the English Bulldog was bred for the same purposes as the Bullenbeisser. This crossing of the two breeds introduced white and particolored or "check" dogs, and was the foundation of the Boxer breed as it is known today.

Development of the Breed

The German Boxer Klub relates that the first reference to the Boxer as a breed occurred as early as 1860 or 1870. The reason for giving a German breed an English name never has been totally understood, though some have theorized that the name stems from the dog's unique use of its forelegs when fighting. Boxers today still display this trait and will try to wrap their strong forelegs around the Schutzhund "helper" (bad guy) when commanded to attack.

In 1895 the German Boxer Klub (Boxer-Klub e.v. Sitz München) was formed in Munich, Germany. The newly formed club developed a breed standard to better define what a Boxer should look like, since in the early days there was much variety in type and style. A dog show was held soon thereafter, and efforts to breed a Boxer conforming to the idealized standard began in earnest.

It is interesting to note that historical photos show that a large number—if not a majority—of early Boxers were either white in color or predominantly white with patches of color. In 1925 white and "check" Boxers were declared unacceptable for registration and showing. One theory regarding this change in heart over acceptable and disqualifying colors is that the decision was influenced by Boxer breeders and perhaps government officials to maximize the number of Boxers eligible for police and military service. To put it simply, white Boxers could be seen at night and dark Boxers could not. If the numbers of solid or near solid fawn and brindle dogs could be increased, and the numbers of white Boxers decreased, the police and military forces would have more Boxers eligible for service.

A look at the Boxers registered in the first decade of the breed shows a dog that looks quite different from today's highly refined breed. Early Boxers were thicker in build, longer in body, and coarser in the head. Within 20 years, however, the outline of today's Boxer began to emerge. With the herculean efforts of German breeders such as

One theory behind the Boxer's name is its unique use of its forearms when fighting.

Observe how this Boxer "hugs" the Schutzhund helper as it bites in practice.

Friederun Stockmann (1891–1972) and her kennels, "vom Dom" (translated as "from the Cathedral"), Germany was able to quickly develop uniformity within the breed and a dog that more closely conformed to the breed standard, or perfection.

However, it wasn't easy for Stockmann and other devoted Boxer breeders to accomplish this task. During World War I, Stockmann relates in her book, *My Life with Boxers,* that there was a severe food shortage and it was a constant hardship to feed her dogs. She describes searching for scraps to feed them by digging through garbage cans at the military barracks. She once bicycled more than 10 miles to pick up a half bucket of intestines. Other times she was forced to do the unspeakable: Feed dog meat to her very own dogs. When her bicycle tires wore out, she wrote that she used braided feathers.

Though the Boxers working on the front lines ate better than those left behind, the Boxers at home were in many ways the lucky ones. Working Boxers suffered heavy casualties during WWI. Keep in mind that these dogs included some of Germany's very best Boxers from the finest kennels. Stockmann relates in her book that her husband, Philip, who organized the training and placement of Boxers as war dogs, took ten dogs with him and returned with only one. The ravages of war were devastating to Germany's supply of Boxers.

The first war was followed by a period of tremendous inflation and a bad situation became even worse. Food was again in extreme shortage. Also, Boxers that had survived the first war were often sterile. Of the litters that were born, there was a high mortality rate. Just when German breeders were beginning to recover, they would be hit with another extreme setback. When it became clear that a second war was imminent, Stockmann wrote that many breeders sold and shipped their Boxers out of the country. A large number of dogs were reportedly killed in advance of any suffering.

When WWII did finally break out, it was equally as devastating to German Boxer breeders and their dogs as World War I. Frau Stockmann wrote that dogs were tested and qualified for their abilities to perform as war dogs and then were whisked off, never to be seen again, leaving owners to guess at their beloved dogs' fates. Only dogs that had passed the rigorous tests in obedience, tracking, messenger, and protection work were given a sort of meal ticket that allowed these Boxers to receive food. With severe food shortages everywhere, this was a particularly important allowance to have for the dogs. It also meant that Boxer breeders worked very hard to make sure all their dogs passed the tests in order to have access to food.

My Life with Boxers

For many years, finding a copy of an out-of-print English translation of Frau Stockmann's book, *My Life with Boxers,* was literally impossible. Fortunately for Boxer fanciers, this incredible book is again available. The new volume is a translation by Calvin Gruver from the third German edition of *Ein Leben mit Boxern.*

This book chronicles Stockmann's life with her Boxers and the almost insurmountable hardships she and her Boxers survived. The book is available with a $100 donation to the American Boxer Charitable Foundation, Inc., a nonprofit division of the American Boxer Club that funds research on life-threatening diseases affecting the Boxer.

Donations should be directed to: American Boxer Charitable Foundation, P.O. Box 300, Rockwood, Michigan 48173-0300; fax: (734) 692-8991.

In addition to being recognized as one of Germany's foremost breeders during the Boxer's formative years, Frau Stockmann was also known for her wood carvings. Here a Boxer is shown is a classic, playful bow with a ball.

It wasn't until years after the conclusion of World War II that the Boxer in Germany would regain its foothold and continue its long tradition of excellence.

Service to Mankind

As mentioned earlier, the Boxer's ancestors served their masters by hunting wild boar and later working as butchers' dogs. When the war began in Germany, the Boxer's duties took another turn.

During World War I, Boxers were part of the 50,000 dogs that were trained and combat-ready in Germany. During the course of the war, Boxers were employed in a variety of jobs. Some Boxers served as guards, making sure that while standing in line, POWs weren't able to pass information to civilians. Boxers were also used to halt smuggling into and out of the country and on the front lines to detect the enemy, alerting the handler by growling softly. Still others were trained to attack anyone who shot at their handlers.

Messenger dogs, or couriers, were trained to carry messages in tubes on their collars. The dogs had to be able to travel long distances quietly and without barking while in enemy fire. In a related duty, war dogs were also called upon to carry a roll of telephone or telegraph wire to link one point to another. Boxers assigned to patrol work were sure footed and became noted for their uncanny ability to lead their handlers along routes even when the handlers did not know their way.

Ambulance Dogs

One of the most interesting facets of war work was the medic or ambulance dog. During World War I, Boxers were trained to seek out wounded soldiers, bite off the soldier's tag, and return to lead a medic to the soldier. One Boxer that was trained to perform this duty saved so many lives during the war that it was awarded Germany's highest honor, the Iron Cross. The female Boxer, Matthias vom Westen, was one of the Stockmann's dogs; however, the German Boxer Klub's records are unclear as to whether Philip Stockmann himself handled the dog, or if it was another soldier. Matthias' war effort is a tribute to this breed's bravery and dedication to the task at hand under the most frightening conditions.

U.S. War Dogs

The Boxer also had an influence in the war effort on the other side of the ocean. Although the United States did not have a canine corps (they were lucky if they were able to use French, Belgian, and English war dogs), there is one American dog that was promoted to "honorary sergeant" by the U.S. Army for its service during the war. Stubby, so named for his docked tail, reportedly was a homeless Boxer or Boxer-cross (there may have been a Bull Terrier involved, according to companion animal historian and author Mary Elizabeth Thurston in *The Lost History of the Canine Race*).

Stubby is credited with saving his regiment many times by alerting the men to incoming mortar shells. A fine sense of smell also enabled Stubby to warn the men of mustard gas and he barked furiously until they put on their gas masks. (Stubby had his own gas mask that the regiment had crafted just for the dog.) Though Stubby perhaps was not a purebred Boxer, he certainly possessed the valiant heart of this breed.

After World War I, the United States developed a K-9 Corps that included Boxers in its initial 32 breeds advocated for military work. The Boxer was also showcased in Dogs for Defense promotional posters in which a soldier and his Boxer were illustrated along with the words: "War Dogs for Our Armed Forces. Give Dogs and Dollars to Dogs for Defense." By the end of World War II, Boxers had served valiantly; however, German Shepherd Dogs had become the dog of choice.

After World War I in Germany

Specific breeds of dogs were approved for police and military work in Germany. Interestingly, even though the Boxer reportedly was the first breed of dog used in the war, it was not approved for police and military service until 1921. The seven breeds that were first approved for police and military service were the Airedale, Boxer, Doberman Pinscher, German Shepherd Dog, Giant Schnauzer, Hovawart, and Rottweiler. The Belgian Malinois and Bouvier were added at a later date;

other breeds such as the Labrador Retriever and some mixed breeds are used by Customs as narcotics search dogs.

In December, 1940, the German government required that all potential military dogs were to be tested for their ability to perform this type of work. Those dogs that passed would be registered for future service and would be allowed to breed in the meantime. Dogs that passed the test were also issued a rationing card for dog food. Records show that 32 percent of all Boxers tested passed. The only breed to have a higher passing percentage was the Airedale Terrier with 33 percent.

Stockmann relates that at the conclusion of World War II, German Shepherd Dogs became the most popular dog of the military. She credits this preference to the fact that German Shepherd Dogs have a thick coat and can survive in much more bitter weather than the smooth-coated Boxer. She also noted that the German Shepherd Dog was easier to train than the Boxer and didn't require as experienced a handler.

Service Work Today

The Boxer today remains a top choice in many areas of service work. It is still an accepted breed for police work in Germany, and despite the common saying that "in the time it takes to train one Boxer, you can train two German Shepherds," Boxers are still trained from time to time as police dogs. They are also used quite successfully as search and rescue dogs for the Red Cross.

In the United States, Boxers are used as drug detection dogs and as search and rescue dogs. They also are frequently trained to work as service dogs, such as seeing eye dogs, hearing dogs, or assistance dogs. Many Boxer owners are involved with their dogs in volunteer pet visitation or animal-assisted therapy work, and thus spread "Boxer love" to an even greater audience.

Without a doubt, the Boxer continues to amaze its owners and handlers with the great breadth of work and service it can provide to humans. Perhaps the only limit to this breed is not with the dog itself, but in the caliber of its handler. In the right hands and with the proper instruction, the Boxer can and still does perform in a great variety of fields. And, as always, it understands how to "turn it on" and "turn

To be eligible for a coveted Sieger title, a German Boxer must have more than just good looks, it must also be titled in Schutzhund.

it off," so even the working Boxer remains a beloved pet at home.

Introduction to America

The first Boxer to achieve a championship from the American Kennel Club (AKC) was rightfully a Boxer from Frau Stockmann's vom Dom kennels. A German champion or "Sieger," Dampf v Dom, owned by the governor of New York and his wife, finished his American championship in 1915. A few fanciers of the breed began forming in the Midwest during the 1920s, but it was not until the early 1930s that the breed really began its sweep across the country.

German Siegers were being imported and campaigned at shows, creating quite a stir among dog fanciers. As more people became familiar with the breed—and as more Boxers were awarded Best in Shows (BIS)—the popularity of the breed also continued to grow. In 1934 a powerful fawn male, International Champion Sigurd v Dom, was imported from Frau Stockmann's kennel, and began to set a few records of his own here. Along with two BIS, 43 Group Firsts, and 54 Best of Breed (BOB)—including one at Westminster Kennel Club's dog show in 1935—Sigurd also was recognized as a leading sire in the United States for many years.

In May, 1935, the American Boxer Club (ABC) was approved by the

AKC as a parent club for the Boxer. At the time, the ABC consisted of just 17 members. The Boxer was initially lumped into the Non-sporting group, but after petitioning the AKC, the Boxer was moved to the Working group where it belonged.

An item of great controversy among this small but growing breed club was the breed standard. Apparently, either a pre-1920 version of the German standard was translated into English and published, or an older Austrian standard was used. Therefore, the first standard that was adopted by the ABC was *not* the current German standard. The result was that the dogs that were being imported from Germany into the United States and those that were being bred, did not conform to the standard. In 1938 the breed standard was revised, with the help of Philip Stockmann, who came to New York City to judge Boxers at Westminster in February, to more closely match the current German standard. The ABC now had more than 100 members. The largest Boxer kennel at the time was Mazelaine, owned by John Wagner. This kennel sometimes had anywhere from 80 to 100 Boxers.

The rest, as we say, is history. Even as U.S. involvement in World War II loomed, Boxer fever had already grabbed dog fanciers across the country and eventually would spread around the world. Many notable kennels would shine in the show ring and rack up honors and awards; to attempt to mention them here would require another book unto itself. However, any book on the Boxer would be remiss not to include one particular dog that is considered by many to be the changing force in American Boxer history: Ch. Bang Away of Sirrah Crest.

Bang Away of Sirrah Crest

In 1939 a doctor and his wife decided they wanted to become serious about breeding Boxers and founded a kennel in California called Sirrah Crest. Little did anyone know at the time that Dr. R. C. Harris and his wife, Phoebe, would breed the most winning Boxer of the century. ("Sirrah" is "Harris" spelled backward.) Purchasing two puppies from Wagner's Mazelaine kennel, the Harrises began their breeding program. In 1949 Bang Away of Sirrah Crest was born. Later that year, Frau Stockmann would visit the United States and would select the flashy fawn and white two-and-a-half-month old Boxer as Best in Match at a local puppy match. Stockmann pronounced that Bang Away would become America's greatest Boxer—and he did. In six years Bang Away had won 121 Best in Show wins, including the coveted Westminster win.

Bang Away is credited with more than just a phenomenal number of wins and in bringing the popularity of Boxers to the top for more than a decade. Bang Away also brought striking style and a certain grace to the breed that is reflected even today in the nation's top Boxers.

Chapter Two
The Boxer Today

The Boxer today is a beautiful animal. It is both powerful and graceful, as well as penetratingly intelligent and whimsical. Though its roots remain in Germany, the Boxer has developed in the United States into its own outstanding version of a universally popular breed. It continues to be a ringside favorite at dog shows, and is adored by breed fanciers and the general dog-loving population alike.

Breed Standard

The following breed standard was revised by the American Boxer Club (ABC) in 1999. The standard is a description of the perfect Boxer. This Boxer, of course, has never existed, but breeders use the standard as a road map in developing their dogs. Occasionally the road map changes, too, as tastes in the United States change. For the most part, however, the standard is very similar to the first German standard upon which it is based.

General Appearance
The *ideal* Boxer is a medium-sized, square built dog of good sub-stance with short back, strong limbs, and short, tight-fitting coat. His well developed muscles are clean, hard and appear smooth under taut skin. His movements denote energy. The gait is firm, yet elastic, the stride freehand ground-covering, the carriage proud. Developed to serve as guard, working and companion dog, he combines strength and agility with elegance and style. His expression is alert and temperament steadfast and tractable. The chiseled head imparts to the Boxer a unique individual stamp. It must be in correct proportion to the body. The broad, blunt muzzle is the distinctive feature, and great value is placed upon its being of proper form and balance with the skull. Indulging the Boxer, first consideration is given to general appearance to which attractive color and arresting style contribute. Next is overall balance with special attention devoted to the head, after which the individual body components are examined for their correct construction, and the efficiency of gait is evaluated.

Size, Proportion, Substance
Height—Adult males 22½ to 25 inches; females 21 to 23½ inches at

the withers, preferably, males should not be under the minimum nor females over the maximum: however, proper balance and quality in the individual should be of primary importance since there is no size disqualification. *Proportion*—The body in profile is of square proportion in that a horizontal line from the front of the forechest to the rear projection of the upper thigh should equal the length of a vertical line dropped from the top of the withers to the ground. *Substance*—Sturdy with **balanced musculature.** Males larger boned than their female counterparts.

Head

The beauty of the head depends upon harmonious proportion of muzzle to skull. The blunt muzzle is ⅓ the length of the head from the occiput to the tip of the nose, and ⅔ the width of the skull. The head should be clean, not showing deep wrinkles (wet). Wrinkles typically appear upon the forehead when ears are erect, and folds are always present from the lower edge of the stop running downward on both sides of the muzzle. *Expression*—Intelligent and alert. *Eyes*—Dark brown in color, not too small, too protruding or too deep-set. Their mood-mirroring character combined with the wrinkling of the forehead, gives the Boxer head its unique quality of expressiveness. *Ears*—Set at the highest point of the sides of the skull are cropped, cut rather long and tapering, raised when alert. *Skull*—The top of the skull is

Today's Boxer commands attention with its intelligent eyes and chiseled body.

slightly arched, not rounded, flat nor noticeably broad, with the occiput not overly pronounced. The forehead shows a slight indentation between the eyes and forms a distinct stop with the topline of the muzzle. The cheeks should be relatively flat and not bulge (cheekiness), maintaining the clean lines of the skull and should taper into the muzzle in a

Regardless of how a Boxer's conformation stacks up, the Boxer is a popular breed worldwide and one of America's favorite house pets.

slight, graceful curve. *Muzzle*—The muzzle, proportionately developed in length, width and depth, has a shape influenced first through the formation of both jawbones, second through the placement of the teeth, and third through the texture of the lips. The top of the muzzle should not slant down (downfaced), nor should it be concave (dishfaced); however, the tip of the nose should lie slightly higher than the root of the muzzle.

The nose should be broad and black.

The upper jaw is broad where attached to the skull and maintains this breadth except for a very slight tapering to the front. The lips, which complete the formation of the muzzle, should meet evenly in front. The upper lip is thick and padded, filling out the frontal space created by the projection of the lower jaw, and laterally is supported by the canines of the lower jaw. Therefore, these canines must stand far apart and be of good length so that the front surface of the muzzle is broad and squarish and, when viewed from the side, shows moderate layback. The chin should be perceptible from the side as well as from the front. *Bite*— The Boxer bite is undershot; the lower jaw protrudes beyond the upper and curves slightly upward. The incisor teeth of the lower jaw are in a straight line, with the canines preferably up front in the same line to give the jaw the greatest possible width. The upper line of incisors is slightly convex with the corner upper incisors fitting snugly back of the lower canine teeth on each side. *Faults*—Skull too broad. Cheekiness. Wrinkling too deep (wet) or lacking (dry). Excessive flews. Muzzle too light for skull. Too pointed a bite (snipy), too undershot, teeth or tongue showing when mouth closed. Eyes noticeably lighter than ground color of coat.

Neck, Topline, Body

Neck—Round, of ample length, muscular and clean without excessive hanging skin (dewlap). The neck has a distinctly marked nape with an elegant arch blending smoothly into

The Boxer combines strength and agility with elegance and style.

the withers. *Topline*—Smooth, firm and slightly sloping. *Body*—The chest is of fair width, and the forechest well defined and visible from the side. The brisket is deep, reaching down to the elbows; the depth of the body at the lowest point of the brisket equals half the height of the dog at the withers. The ribs, extending far to the rear, are well arched but not barrel shaped. The back is short, straight and muscular and firmly connects the withers to the hindquarters.

The loins are short and muscular. The lower line is slightly tucked up, blending into a graceful curve to the rear. The coup is slightly sloped, flat and broad. Tail is set high, docked and carried upward. Pelvis long and in females especially broad. *Faults*—Short heavy neck. Chest too broad,

too narrow or hanging between the shoulders. Lack of forechest. Hanging stomach. Slab-sided rib cage. Long or narrow loin, weak union with croup. Falling off of croup. Higher in rear than in front.

Forequarters

The shoulders are long and sloping, close-lying, and not excessively covered with muscle (loaded). The upper arm is long, approaching a right angle to the shoulder blade. The elbows should not press too closely to the chest wall nor stand off visibly from it.

The forelegs are long, straight and firmly muscled and when viewed from the front, stand parallel to each other. The pastern is strong and distinct, slightly slanting, but standing almost perpendicular to the ground. The dewclaws may be removed. Feet should be compact, turning neither in nor out, with well arched toes. *Faults*—Loose or loaded shoulders. Tied in or bowed out elbows.

Hindquarters

The hindquarters are strongly muscled with angulation in balance with that of the forequarters.

The thighs are broad and curved, the breech musculature hard and strongly developed. Upper and lower thigh long. Leg well angulated at the stifle with a clearly defined, well "let down" hock joint. Viewed from behind, the hind legs should be straight with hock joints leaning neither in nor out. From the side, the leg below the hock (metatarsus) should be almost perpendicular to the ground, with a slight slope to the rear permissible. The metatarsus should be short, clean and strong. The Boxer has no rear dewclaws. Faults—Steep or over-angulated hindquarters. Light thighs or overdeveloped hams. Over-angulated (sickle) hocks. Hindquarters too far under or too far behind.

Coat

Short, shiny, lying smooth and tight to the body.

White markings on the coat enhance the Boxer's appearance.

Color

The colors are fawn and brindle. Fawn shades vary from light tan to mahogany. The brindle ranges from sparse, but clearly defined black stripes on a fawn background, to such a heavy concentration of black striping that the essential fawn background color barely, although clearly, shows through (which may create the appearance of "reverse brindling").

White markings should be of such distribution as to enhance the dog's appearance, but may not exceed one-third of the entire coat. They are not desirable on the flanks or on the back of the torso proper. On the face, white may replace part of the otherwise essential black mask and may extend in an upward path between the eyes, but it must not be excessive, so as to detract from true Boxer expression. *Faults*—Unattractive or misplaced white markings. *Disqualifications*—Boxers that are any color other than fawn or brindle. Boxers with a total of white markings exceeding one-third of the entire coat.

Gait

Viewed from the side, proper front and rear angulation is manifested in a smoothly efficient level-backed, ground covering stride with powerful drive emanating from a freely operating rear. Although the front legs do not contribute impelling power, adequate "reach" should be evident to prevent interference, overlap or "sidewinding" (crabbing).

Viewed from the front, the shoulders should remain trim and the elbows not flare out. The legs are parallel until gaiting narrows the track in proportion to increasing speed, then the legs come in under the body but should never cross. The line from the shoulder down through the leg should remain straight although not necessarily perpendicular to the ground. Viewed from the rear, a Boxer's rump should not roll. The hind feet should "dig in" and track relatively true with the front. Again, as speed increases, the normally broad rear track will become narrower. *Faults*—Stilted or inefficient gait. Lack of smoothness.

Character and Temperament

These are of paramount importance in the Boxer. Instinctively a "hearing" guard dog, his bearing is alert, dignified and self-assured. In the show ring, his behavior should exhibit constrained animation. With family and friends, his temperament is fundamentally playful, yet patient and stoical with children. Deliberate and wary with strangers, he will exhibit curiosity but, most importantly, fearless courage if threatened. However, he responds promptly to friendly overtures honestly rendered. His intelligence, loyal affection and tractability to discipline make him a highly desirable companion. *Faults*—Lack of dignity and alertness. Shyness.

The foregoing description is that of the ideal Boxer. Any deviations from the above described dog must be penalized to the extent of the deviation.

Disqualifications

Boxers that are any color other than fawn or brindle. Boxers with a total of white markings exceeding one-third of the entire coat.

Approved February 5, 1999
Effective March 31, 1999
Reprinted courtesy of the American Boxer Club.

The Boxer in Other Countries

As mentioned earlier, over the last century the Boxer has evolved into an extremely popular dog in the United States. In England the Boxer is very similar, but it too has developed into a slightly different animal. Australian and Japanese Boxers also have a bit of uniqueness to them. There's no question that regardless of the country of origin, a Boxer is a Boxer; however, it is interesting to see how members of different countries and cultures view the "perfect" Boxer.

Perhaps the most striking difference in conformation in the Boxer is seen in the home of the breed itself, Germany. Here, a strong emphasis on breeding working dogs has influenced the development of the breed, which is larger boned, more heavily muscled, broader in head, and shorter in muzzle than its North American counterparts. The German Boxer's consistently outstanding performance in tracking, obedience,

The German Boxer is slightly different in conformation from its American counterpart and is required to pass rigorous health, endurance, training, and conformation tests prior to being given approval by the German Boxer Klub to be bred.

and protection work is also noticeable. (In Germany, Boxers are still actively used in police and military work.) German breeders also relate an extremely low incidence of white Boxers, and relatively few health problems.

But breeders are quick to point out that the German Boxer wasn't always this way and that heart disorders and hip dysplasia plagued the breed in the 1960s. The introduction of the Zuchttauglichkeitsprüfung (ZTP or breeding qualification test) enabled the Boxer Klub of Germany to maintain minimum breeding requirements. The ZTP is credited with wiping out much of the German Boxer's health, temperament, and conformation problems.

ZTP

The ZTP was introduced in Germany in the late 1940s as an optional test to substantiate a Boxer's suitability for breeding. The test, which examines the Boxer's conformation, health, temperament, and working abilities, became a mandatory test for all Boxers seeking approval for breeding in 1974. Boxers that pass the rigorous ZTP have their test results recorded and are then allowed to be bred. Any Boxer that does *not* pass the ZTP (only two chances are given) is proclaimed "Zuchtverbot" and cannot be bred—ever. If it is, the puppies are not allowed to be registered. In the United States, this would be

The long show crop favored by American Boxer fanciers is not allowed in England, Germany, and several European countries.

similar to denying a Boxer the ability to register as a purebred; it would be "paperless."

The ZTP is constructed of three separate tests in which the Boxer must be graded: health, conformation, and temperament.

Health

In the health section of the test, the Boxer must be x-rayed for hip dysplasia and receive certification that it is free of it.

Note: Boxers with ratings of "transition" or "slight" are able to test for the ZTP; however, if they pass, these dogs must be bred to a Boxer that is

The Boxer is a working dog and maintains its strength today through Schutzhund.

members in dealing with heart problems. They want more. Currently, the Boxer Klub is encouraging owners to test their dogs for AS and other heart diseases. The test results are then recorded permanently on the dog's records and on any future pedigrees. The Klub hopes to make heart testing a mandatory part of the ZTP in the future.

Another health test that is being promoted by the Boxer Klub is the spinal X ray to detect spondylosis, a degenerative disease of the spine. Again, Klub members are mixed as to whether they want this test to be added to the long list of requirements for breeding registration; however, the Klub reports its membership is for the most part supportive of including this test in the ZTP.

Conformation

Once the Boxer has passed all necessary health tests, it must now be presented to a judge to be graded in 63 different categories of conformation. Literally every aspect of the dog, from its eye color and tooth formation to its paws, is graded on a scale of one to five, with the number three position being the most favorable. Few Boxers fail the conformation exam because, as one longtime breeder noted, owners know if their dogs can pass or not and if they can't, the owner doesn't attempt the ZTP.

Temperament

The final phase of the ZTP is the temperament test in which the Boxer

certified clear of the disease. Next, the Boxer is tested for its endurance through a 12.4-mile (20-km) trot alongside a bicycle, which is traveling roughly 7½ to 9 miles an hour (12 to 15 km/hour). The endurance test is used to prove the stamina of the Boxer—vital to a working dog—and to weed out "bad" hearts. Since the prevalent heart disorder in Germany is aortic stenosis (AS) rather than Boxer cardiomyopathy, Boxers with AS would likely have difficulties with this portion of the test (for more on these heart diseases, see Chapter Eleven).

The endurance test, however, is not considered sufficient by some

is tested on its steadiness, protection abilities, and courage in a sort of "mini" Schutzhund test. For German Boxer owners, it is important for the heritage of the breed that Boxers retain their original temperament and prove they are good "Schutzdienst" (Schutzhund test takers).

1. In the steadiness portion of the test, the Boxer must walk on a relaxed leash alongside its owner and remain steady when, with no warning, a person fires off a gun at close range. The dog may not show fearfulness or aggressiveness.

2. In the protection portion of the temperament test, the Boxer is taken across a field—more than 50 yards (46 m)—by a person other than the dog's owner. The dog then watches as a person pretends to leap out and suddenly attack the dog's owner. The Boxer is released and, with no commands, must run down the attacker, bite the specially padded arm, and hold the bite until the owner gives the command "aus!" (out). The dog must then sit with no further biting or barking.

3. In the final section of the ZTP, the Boxer's courage is tested. The helper, a specially trained person who is heavily padded, runs straight for the Boxer and its owner, shouting in a loud, erratic, and menacing manner. On command, the Boxer must run to the attacker and bite the helper's arm. The dog must hold the arm—it's padded—until the owner can run to the dog and give it the *out* command and put it into a controlled *sit*.

Higher Titles and Red Papers

If this sounds like a lot of work to go through to be able to breed a dog, it is, but, to achieve an even higher status as a Boxer, the dog must go through additional tests. To achieve the advanced level of "Körung," the Boxer must attain a Schutzhund title (Schutzhund involves obedience, tracking, and protection work), and must receive two "very good" ratings at two different dog shows. In Germany, all dogs are judged against the standard in the show ring and receive a rating *at each show,* along with a copy of the judge's comments for that particular dog. Owning a Köered Boxer is important for two reasons. First, it allows the Boxer to be bred to *any* Boxer that has passed its ZTP. Second, it can now be selected to win special "winner" or "Sieger" titles at shows.

Restrictions in America?

Though interest groups have from time to time attempted to convince breeders that minimum health standards should be set in order for dogs to be bred in the United States, it is unlikely that American Boxer breeders would submit to the extensive restrictions presented by Germany's breeding requirements. However, there have been inroads made toward providing puppy buyers with similar information.

If a breeder permanently identifies his or her Boxers through microchipping or tattooing, the American Kennel Club will record the results of certain health tests and screenings with the dog's records. Conformation championships have always been recorded with the dog's information, as are performance event titles awarded in AKC events. All these records help to give the puppy buyer an indication of the background of their puppy, but the burden of finding out if a puppy comes from healthy stock with excellent conformation still weighs on the buyer.

This check Boxer is most likely oblivious to the issues surrounding its color.

Controversial Issues Facing the Breed

Every breed has its issues. How a breed club handles these issues, however, can greatly affect how the breed develops in the future. For the Boxer, there are three issues that are currently of interest to many fanciers: the white Boxer, cropped ears, and docked tails.

The White Boxer

In the early days of the breed, the Boxer came in many colors, including a large percentage of white and particolor or check dogs. Until World War I the colors of white and particolor were accepted by the German Boxer Klub. It is thought that during the war, however, the acceptance of this color fell out of favor when it was discovered that a white messenger dog was much more visible at night than a darkly colored dog. In 1925 white Boxers were ousted from the stud books, allowed back in temporarily in the 1930s, and then never accepted as an allowable color in that country again.

In the United States, the standard has always read that a dog with too much white possesses a disqualifying fault. Unfortunately, for years the American Boxer Club took a rather harsh stand on what to do with puppies that had this disqualifying fault. Club members were not allowed to sell, place, or breed a white Boxer. This left breeders faced with the decision either of keeping all the white puppies from every litter they bred, or euthanizing them. Neither choice was acceptable to many breeders, particularly when as much as 25 percent of every litter is white.

In the late 1990s the winds began to change. The ABC revised its restrictions to allow owners to place their white puppies, but maintained that the puppies could not be sold, registered, or bred. For many breeders, this was just the relaxation in the rule they were looking for.

Others, however, are looking for more. There are fanciers of white Boxers who would like to see the white Boxer accepted as an allowable color in the breed standard. They would also like to see the white Boxer used in breeding programs. This would be difficult, warn critics of the movement, because the white coat color is linked to genetic deafness, which would add one more health issue for breeders to worry about. Other breeders note that though they abide by the ABC's rule on white Boxers, they're not sure that summarily eliminating white Boxers from breeding programs isn't eliminating some of the best dogs.

Currently, white Boxer owners can get Indefinite Listing Privilege (see page 61 for an explanation of ILP) numbers for their dogs and compete in many of the AKC's performance events. Though the white Boxer is not in the show ring, it has made a permanent spot for itself in the hearts and homes of Boxer owners across the country.

Cropped Ears

To achieve the permanently erect ear of the Boxer, the ear must be trimmed to a point and the edges stitched to close the wound. The ears must then be taped and put in a rack so that they heal in the proper position and don't flop. The procedure is performed by a veterinarian with the Boxer under an anesthetic.

Ear cropping is considered major surgery and may involve one to two months of meticulous medical aftercare to heal properly and in the correct position.

The breed's ears have been cropped in this fashion since the beginning of the breed. Since the late 1980s, however, it has been illegal in many countries to crop a dog's ears. (German Boxers have been sporting natural ears for more than a decade.)

In the United States, an increasing number of pet owners are not cropping their dogs' ears either because they favor the look of the natural ear, or they simply don't want to spend the money and time necessary to insure that the cropped ears will heal correctly.

In the show ring, it was virtually unheard of to present a Boxer without cropped ears, but there are now several champions that were finished with natural ears, and there are factions of Boxer owners and non-Boxer owners that are pushing to ban cropped ears in the United States. The breed standard that was released in 1999, however, states that the ears should be cropped. Perhaps in the future this will be relaxed to allow both cropped and uncropped dogs to be shown without penalization.

Docked Tails

It seems that changes always affect the Boxers overseas first, and the repercussions of these changes then gradually ripple across the Atlantic to the United States. The latest controversy to hit Europe—and one that Boxer owners in this country are keeping an eye on—is that of the undocked tail. Boxer tails are generally docked by a veterinarian within the first few days following the puppies' birth. This is not so anymore in many European countries where tail docking has been banned and the Boxer is now sporting a full tail.

Yes, a Boxer wagging a full tail does look a bit different. It doesn't look bad, mind you, just very different. Though there have been no movements within the ABC to allow undocked tails, who knows what the future will hold? If Boxers are allowed to have their tails at some date, watch out! This is a tail with one muscular whip to it and given the Boxer's joyful temperament, the greatest concern of owners may be in their own personal safety.

Chapter Three

The Boxer as a Companion

There are many reasons why the Boxer has been a consistent favorite with Americans and Canadians:

• It is a versatile breed that can adapt to many different living environments.
• It can and does do well at most anything.
• It excels at performance events just as much as it excels at being a favorite house pet.
• It will entertain and love a family of five, or be quite content as an "only child" of someone who is single.
• Finally, the Boxer is a strikingly handsome animal. It is virtually impossible to walk a well-cared-for Boxer without turning heads and being stopped by admiring dog lovers.

But the Boxer is not without its faults—or "challenges," as breed lovers would prefer to call them. So, before you make the decision to purchase a Boxer as your canine companion, it is important to balance the breed's strengths with its potential foibles. For many Boxers owners, the challenges of owning and caring for the breed that are listed in this chapter are considered minor and are readily accepted as part of the whole package. For other dog owners, however, what might be considered no big deal to a Boxer lover could be considered unbearable to someone who has not previously owned the breed.

Boxer Strengths

As mentioned above, the Boxer is a good-looking dog. A well-fed, conditioned Boxer has a glossy coat, well-defined muscles, and alert, penetrating eyes. The Boxer is attractive and varied in coloring as well, coming in a wide range of fawns and brindles, often with flashy white markings on the chest, neck, legs, and head—no two Boxers look alike. The short coat of the Boxer requires minimal care to keep it looking sleek.

Love of Family

But, of course, the strengths of the Boxer go much deeper than its

appearance. The Boxer is a very loyal, family-oriented dog. It is a natural watchdog to members of its family, and will bark quite furiously when a stranger comes to the door, but it is not normally an aggressive dog toward people. Once the visitor is invited into the home, a Boxer will revert from barking to furiously wagging its little docked tail.

Boxers enjoy being involved in everyday family life and, as a whole, love their families dearly. They make excellent pets for older children, or those children who don't mind a good-hearted bowling over on occasion from an exuberant dog. Very small children should be supervised, simply because the dog's size and strength could accidently cause a small child to have a rather hard tumble.

The temperament of the Boxer is one that has not been diluted with its popularity. It remains a very loyal, even-tempered, gentle breed that maintains its good sense even when treated very poorly. National Boxer Rescue estimates that less than 1 percent of the more than 1,000 Boxers that have been rescued—many from dire situations of filth, starvation, and/or cruelty—have had to be euthanized due to a poor temperament with people. In dogs that are raised in nurturing environments, the number of ill-tempered Boxers is thought to be even less.

Trainability

The Boxer is a very intelligent dog that is quite trainable. It thoroughly enjoys any and all opportunities to be with its master, and that includes daily training sessions. The versatility and athleticism of the breed also make it a good choice for a variety of competitive sports. Boxers are natural obedience dogs, and also perform well in agility, flyball, disk competitions, and Schutzhund.

Compatability with Other Pets

And finally, the Boxer usually does well as a second pet with other Boxers, and other breeds of dogs. In fact, two Boxers can be better than one; an active playmate can keep the Boxer from becoming bored and destructive. If an owner is considering

Though the Boxer is touted as a tremendous kids' dog, both dog and child must be taught to respect each other.

Any time is playtime for a Boxer.

these other pets as a puppy. Adult Boxers may even succeed with cats if the cat's claws are intact and the cat is of the temperament that allows it to put the Boxer in its place.

Boxer Challenges

The Boxer is a wonderful dog, but no breed of dog is perfect; Boxers have their imperfections, too. Often, new Boxer owners quickly find that the challenges of owning a Boxer fall into one of three categories:

1. cute, endearing and forgivable
2. slightly annoying but workable
3. totally incompatible.

How you categorize the challenges of owning a Boxer is an individual decision; however, before buying a Boxer, you should give serious consideration to the breed's less desirable traits, and decide how well you will handle these breed characteristics. Keep in mind, too, that most dog ownership "problems" are solvable if the owner is patient, creative, and willing to make the necessary lifestyle changes to comfortably accommodate his or her canine companion. Following are important points to consider in owning a Boxer.

Training is a must. The Boxer is neither a particularly tall nor heavy dog, but it is extremely strong. Without any conditioning whatsoever, a five-month-old puppy is capable of taking its owner for a not-so-merry romp around the block. A gleeful greeting at the front door from an

owning more than one Boxer, or any dog for that matter, male-female pairings seem to fare the best overall. Male Boxers, particularly if neutered, can live peacefully (and playfully) with other males, and females have been known to get along fine with other females. However, if a Boxer decides it doesn't like a particular Boxer in the home, it may hold a lifelong grudge. In instances such as these, permanent separation will be necessary to prevent either dog from seriously injuring the other.

Boxers also can fare well with other pet species, such as cats and "pocket" pets (hamsters, gerbils, mice), if the Boxer is raised with

unruly adolescent could also easily topple an adult who is less steady on his or her feet. For these reasons, immediate and consistent training is a must. Puppies should be enrolled in puppy kindergarten as soon as their veterinarians give the OK (see page 159). Most veterinarians like to make sure that young puppies have received enough vaccinations to be immune to a variety of common, deadly diseases. Adult dogs that are being adopted should also be enrolled in a training class and the owner should work with the dog daily until it has reached a sufficient level of obedience.

Basic obedience training is the best investment you can make in your Boxer. Sure, it's time-consuming and it does cost money, but once you become involved with your Boxer's training, chances are you'll discover it's a lot of fun. In the long run, training your dog for 10 months to a year will help you achieve a well-behaved, welcome member of the family. If your puppy or dog is cherished, owning it will be a pleasure, not a pain.

The Boxer's activity level can be high. If you are used to a dog that gently wags its tail when you come in the door at night and then takes up its resident spot in front of the hearth, or if you've owned cats that peacefully sleep on the top of your computer monitor and don't even register your existence when you walk in the room, you might find the activity level of the Boxer a little more than you're accustomed to.

Boxers do move around a bit. On a scale of 1 to 10, with "1" being dead and "10" being perpetual, non-stop motion—they're either moving or they're sleeping and they're hardly ever sleeping—the Boxer would range in the 5 to 6 zone. Basically, if the Boxer gets sufficient

The Boxer is a high-energy dog that needs to have its drive channeled into constructive activities.

Boxers are known to be up for any activity as long as it means being closest to you.

exercise throughout the day, it won't drive you crazy. What's a sufficient amount of exercise? A good morning romp, a midday walk, and another evening romp will do just fine. Or, if you don't have a yard in which your dog can really stretch its legs, three, 20-minute vigorous walks should take care of most young and middle-aged dogs.

Regular exercise will take the energetic edge off your dog, but don't expect your Boxer to resign itself to a quiet corner in the room. Once inside, the Boxer will continue to gently, and sometimes not so gently, demand attention. You may find your Boxer following you from room to room and sitting close to you for you to stroke it. Or your Boxer may drop toy after toy at your feet until it can entice you into a game of tug-of-war or indoor catch. Some dog owners find this canine attention annoying; others see it as one of the behaviors that is endearing in the Boxer. How you evaluate this activity level is entirely up to your expectations of what a dog should or shouldn't be. So, if you prefer a dog that is less demonstrative in its affections, a Boxer may not be for you.

Boxers cannot tolerate excessive heat or cold. The Boxer is not an outdoor dog and does not do well in extremely cold or hot weather. Its short, sleek coat will thicken somewhat in cold weather, but it will not develop enough to keep the dog warm for any extended periods of time. In other words, if you have to throw on a winter coat to get the newspaper, it's probably too cold for your Boxer except for those times when it is exercising.

Also, if the temperature is too high, your Boxer will suffer, too. As a

You never know what Boxers will do next, so be prepared for anything.

brachycephalic (short-nosed) breed, the Boxer is less efficient at cooling itself off than other, longer-nosed breeds. It can't tolerate very hot days even if it has a shady place to rest outside. The Boxer also can't be expected to compete in any taxing performance events, such as flyball or agility, on a hot summer day.

Boxers are destructive when bored or lonely. Boxers love their people and do not like to be separated from them for any period of time. If left alone, the Boxer will think of ways to amuse itself, or it will try to rejoin its family. In the backyard, a bored Boxer might choose to dig a trench in your prized rose bed, remove and destroy a newly planted sapling, or simply chew through a wood post in your deck. Inside, the neglected Boxer may decide your windows look better without blinds, or that two carpets, in asymmetrical

sections, fit the room better than one. If the Boxer is outside and wants to come inside to be with you, you could find a screen door off its hinges.

Yes, Boxers have been known to do all of these things and more. A happy Boxer, however, does not do these things. Why? Two reasons. A happy Boxer gets to live with its family. Its activities are supervised and, because it receives lots of interaction and love from humans, the happy Boxer is less likely to become lonely, bored, and destructive. When the Boxer cannot be supervised—for example if the owner is going out to dinner for a few hours—the wise owner makes sure the Boxer is exercised, watered, properly relieved, and then put into its crate with a good chew toy.

Agility takes a toll. The Boxer is very agile and nimble. These admirable qualities, however, can be troublesome if used at the wrong place at the wrong time. For example, the counter-jumping ability of the Boxer can be frustrating when you have company coming in less than five minutes and your Boxer has plucked the cooling roast from your kitchen counter and taken it to the backyard to devour. The dog's agility, coupled with the breed's good sense of smell, makes a situation in which literally nothing is safe on the counters, tabletops, or other "in-reach" surfaces. So, if you're used to leaving bonbons on the coffee table or bread on the kitchen counter, you'll want to find new places for these foods or restrict your Boxer from these irresistible temptations.

Cleverness can be a drawback. Can a dog be too smart for its own good? Perhaps. If so, the Boxer may be a candidate for the canine Mensa club. Boxers can figure out how to open latches, pull open drawers, and even raid refrigerators. They can also be very determined in their cleverness. If at first a Boxer doesn't succeed at getting what it wants, it may try again and again and again—each time in a different way—until it *does* succeed. Boxer owners are generally amused at their dogs' cleverness, but this trait also requires that the owners remain one step ahead of their dogs.

The drawbacks of being a bit too clever can also extend into a Boxer's obedience and performance event training. Since the Boxer learns so quickly, it must be kept interested in the task at hand if it is to continue to perform that task. In other words, if the dog's training is not kept lively and interesting, the Boxer often finds ways to "untrain" itself.

Stubborn streaks: In addition to being quite clever, the Boxer can also be downright stubborn at times. When (not *if*) a stubborn streak appears in a mature Boxer, it takes some determination and patience to work the dog through its "moment." If an owner is not up to the challenge of working a Boxer through a momentary lapse of good sense, a Boxer that is very stubborn could be difficult to handle. For example, when a 70-pound (32 kg) package of canine muscle decides that it *won't* jump into the back of your car, you must know how to be both gentle and firm in convincing your Boxer that, yes, it really must go in the car *now*. Uncorrected stubborn streaks can develop into a tendency to dominate an owner, which must quickly be put to a halt.

Note: This does not imply that a Boxer is aggressive toward its owner. A Boxer that dominates its owner is one that gets what it wants and does what it pleases regardless of what the owner says or does.

Owners that are frail in health or weak in spirit may need to seek professional help in training a more stubborn Boxer to respect them.

Sloppy dinner manners: The Boxer's mouth, teeth, and lips were not designed for black tie dining. Remember, this breed has a jaw that was meant to be able to bite and hold onto its prey or opponent. What this means is that today's Boxer, which retains the physical equipment to bite but is not a "biter" as such, is not a very neat eater. In fact, when a Boxer is eating, it is not a very pretty sight. Boxer owners are used to their dogs' sprinkling of dinner remnants around the food bowl, but owners of neater-eating breeds might be a bit shocked—and perhaps a bit distraught by the amount of after-dinner floor cleaning that is necessary. Drinking water can also be a real event for the un-Boxerized owner. As with any longer-lipped breed, water is often held in the dog's upper hanging lips, and dribbled across the floor as the dog moves away from its bowl.

Drooling: The Boxer is not any worse at drooling than breeds of similar lip construction; however, if you are used to a tight-lipped breed that does not drool at all, and the idea of a dog occasionally drooling when it is excited, when it has just been exercising, or when it spots something it would really like to eat, then you might want to think about this.

Flatulence: Oh yes, and there's this little issue of bad gas. Boxers tend to produce copious amounts of fragrant fumes after they have consumed their meals. This can be quite offensive to owners of more delicate constitutions, but most Boxer owners take it in stride. The reason for the flatulence is believed to be connected to the breed's difficulties digesting soy and soy products.

Much of a dog's after-dinner condition may be controlled through a carefully selected diet.

Health issues: The Boxer as a breed is susceptible to some diseases and conditions that could substantially shorten its life span (see chapter Eleven: Common Diseases of the Boxer). Though many owners accept these risks as part of the Boxer package, and practice as much preventive veterinary care as possible, other dog owners simply don't want to add these worries to dog ownership. Prospective Boxer owners would be well advised to be as educated as possible about these diseases and conditions and make sure they select a puppy or adopt an adult that has the least possible chance of developing problems later in life.

Owners should look for puppies with parents and grandparents, if possible, that have been tested for serious, hereditary diseases such as hip dysplasia, Boxer cardiomyopathy, and subaortic stenosis. Keep in mind, however, that even a dog with generations of documented, healthy, long-lived parentage is no absolute guarantee of perfect health, though it greatly enhances the dog's chances of living a healthy life.

Before You Buy

You've weighed the pros and cons of Boxer ownership and are willing to make the relationship work. Now, you must take a good, hard, and honest look at yourself, your loved ones, and your lifestyle to make sure you can and are able to make the lifestyle changes necessary to create a healthy, nurturing environment for your new Boxer.

Meeting the Boxer

Before you have firmly decided to purchase or adopt a Boxer, take time to visit with Boxer breeders and owners.

• Observe how these Boxer lovers handle their dogs.

• Note how the breed interacts with humans—both familiar and strange. (Be prepared to be licked a *lot*.)

• If you are married, and/or have children, watch how your family members interact with the adult dogs. Everyone loves a puppy, but how do your loved ones respond to a bouncy, playful, 60-pound (27-kg)

There is no breed that can claim to be more loyal or devoted than the heroic Boxer.

red brindle female with cropped ears that kind of looks ferocious? Do your children quickly overcome the appearance of the dog and seem to enjoy being around the dog? Or, do they run for cover?

• If you live in a household of more than one, it is very important for the success of the dog in the home that everyone in that household admires and enjoys the Boxer. There have been far too many rescue stories of households with mixed emotions over the dog. The Boxer usually always loses in these instances and ends up being relinquished to the care of a rescue organization or turned into the local pound. Don't let this be your story!

Evaluating Your Available Time

Do you work long hours at your job? Do you have small children? Are you driving from activity to activity every night of the week? If your time is already thin, you will need to either rearrange your schedule and your priorities, or postpone adding a dog to your life at the present moment. Since daily training and exercise are required with Boxer ownership, you will need to carve out time for these activities. If time is tight and you still want a dog *now,* make sure you have a fat bank account, because you'll need a good supply of cash to make sure a dog walker can give your Boxer the daily exercise it needs, as well as a professional trainer to work with your dog on a daily basis.

Knowing Your Finances

As mentioned above, depending on your situation, dog ownership may be very expensive. On average, the first year of owning a dog can cost more than $2,000—and that's if everything goes well and you don't need any emergency surgeries to patch up torn skin or repair an injured foot. Subsequent years may cost less, but they may not. According to some estimates, an average, healthy midsize dog costs approximately $1,000 a year to maintain. If this is not in your budget, you may want to wait before purchasing a Boxer. This is not a breed that can flourish under poor conditions.

Considering Your Living Arrangements

Are you a homeowner, or do you rent? If you rent, be sure to check the renter's agreement to see whether you are allowed a pet, what the size limits are, and how much the monthly pet fee is *before* you purchase a Boxer. Rental properties frequently restrict renters to a 20-pound (9 kg) dog limit. An adult Boxer does not meet this requirement! Also, many rental properties charge a hefty deposit prior to the arrival of a new pet, as well as a monthly fee as high as $50 a pet or more. You may also be required to provide proof of owning a good dog through letters from previous neighbors and your veterinarian. This can be troublesome for the person who is *buying* a new dog, because providing this type of proof would be impossible.

Another consideration renters should concern themselves with is how often they move. Frequent moves are not impossible if the owner is committed to moving the Boxer as if it were a family member. In some instances, this may mean more extensive house hunting, or even special arrangements to have food shipped, as in temporary overseas moves.

Level of Commitment

Successful dog ownership really boils down to one simple element: the level of commitment of the owner. A committed owner is one that willingly will do whatever it takes to create an environment that is safe, healthy, and happy for his or her Boxer and does not try to skimp or cut corners in the care of the dog. A committed owner is well educated as to the needs and behaviors of the Boxer, and knows how to handle most situations, or is willing to seek advice from experienced Boxer owners. With a committed owner, there really isn't any dog ownership obstacle that can't be overcome by using a little creativity and a lot of determination.

Do You Have What It Takes?

The Boxer is a wonderful breed with many strengths and few weaknesses, but, as previously discussed, it is not a perfect dog and it is definitely not the dog for everyone. And,

Children and Boxers

It is a common misconception that kids and dogs go together like peanut butter and jelly. They don't. Children must be taught how to interact appropriately with a puppy or dog, and the dog must be taught how to behave around children. Boxers are not known to have problems with aggression to people, though there are always rare exceptions, so a cautious parent should *never* entirely rule this out with any dog. Most often, however, injuries to children occur because the Boxer is a big, enthusiastic dog, and is easily capable of accidently toppling a small child. For this reason, parents of young children need to provide continuous, close-range supervision of all dog-child play, or be able to separate the child from the dog during unsupervised times. To do otherwise is inviting an accident to occur.

Training can help a Boxer refrain from hugging everyone it meets, but sometimes a dog just has too much love to contain itself.

even if this *is* the dog for you, the timing may be all wrong. If all the pieces are not in place in your life for you to welcome a Boxer into your home, then hold off on your purchase. Make changes as necessary in your home first. Maybe you need to wait for your little ones to get a little older. Or, perhaps you need to work on scheduling less in your life and making more time for yourself, your family, and later, a new dog. If finances are a sticking point, begin

by stashing some cash in a savings account for the dog's care; just because *now* is not the right time, doesn't mean you can't begin planning for a Boxer in the future.

Of course, if the time is right, and this is the dog for you, you can begin your search for a new Boxer. Whether you decide to purchase a puppy or adopt an adult dog, if you choose carefully and raise your Boxer right, it will very quickly become a loyal and devoted family member.

Can You Afford a Boxer?

Dogs are expensive, and Boxers are no exceptions. The following is a list of expenses you can expect to incur in your first year of owning a Boxer.

Crate (large)	$100
Pad for crate	$50
Baby gates (2)	$80
Pet stain and odor remover (1 gallon [3.8 L])	$20
Various chew toys	$30
"Anti-chewing" spray (16-ounce spray)	$ 7
"Big dog" scoop	$17
Dog food (quality)	$400
Dog bowls (ceramic or no-tip stainless steel) (2)	$20
Dental kit (toothbrush, toothpaste, finger brush)	$6
Adjustable collars (2)	$10
Matching 6-foot (1.8 m) leash	$9
Personalized dog tag	$5
Toenail clippers, styptic powder	$17
Brush	$12
Dog shampoo, conditioner (concentrated; 1 gallon [3.8 L])	$35
Doses of flea and tick control (12)	$72
Heartworm preventive	$120
Routine veterinary care	$200
Obedience classes (10 months)	$200
First Year Total	**$1,410**

Other:

Fencing for yard	$300–$1,000+
Dog door	$100–$250
Boarding, kennel (2-week vacation)	$170
Spay/Neuter	$120–$200+

Chapter Four

Choosing the Best Boxer for You

The Boxer Puppy

There may not be anything more adorable than a Boxer puppy. Its floppy ears, dark eyes, and wrinkled, quizzical looks are enough to melt any dog owner's heart. The breed's flashy coloring in rich fawns and exotic brindles further enhances the attraction to this breed. Mix in the Boxer puppy's propensity to take part in high-energy play, and you

It is very important that your puppy remain with its mother and littermates until it is at least eight weeks old or even older.

have a recipe for a stunning, lovable puppy that is extremely entertaining just to watch. But don't expect to remain a casual observer when there's a Boxer puppy around. These puppies are always up for a good game, no matter what the game or who is playing—and you *will* play!

In a word, Boxer puppies are irresistible. Quick to learn, eager to please, and a wriggly bundle of warmth and love, a Boxer puppy is a delight to be around—at least for a few minutes. Sure, puppies are cute; if they weren't, no human being could put up with the endless chores, home furnishings destruction, sleepless nights, and just plain hard work that is involved in raising a puppy in a healthy and loving environment. That's not to say that raising a puppy doesn't have its delightful moments and lasting rewards, but rearing a puppy into a well-mannered, delightful member of the family takes work and commitment. For many Boxer owners, the benefits of puppy ownership far outweigh the drawbacks. Dog lovers who aren't sure they're quite up to the intensive care of a little puppy, however, may find adopting an adult dog is a better option.

Adopted adult Boxers make wonderful pets and can be less challenging in many ways than a puppy (see Adopting the Adult Boxer, Chapter Five); there are many adults in need of homes. But if a puppy is what you really want, consider making a donation to Boxer Rescue to help those grown-up pups get a second chance on life.

Benefits and Drawbacks of Puppy Ownership

Most Boxer owners buy their dogs as puppies. At the end of the 1990s approximately 13,638 litters of Boxer puppies were registered annually with the American Kennel Club. Assuming an average litter of six, that's roughly 82,000 Boxer puppies born each year. This number is probably on the low side since it reflects only those Boxers whose owners chose to register their litters. It is safe to assume that an equal number of purebred pet-bred Boxer litters are never registered, so the total number of Boxer puppies born each year is closer to 164,000.

Most of these puppies do well in their new homes, but some do not. The American Boxer Rescue Association (ABRA) reports that literally thousands of Boxers—from young

Quality

A reputable breeder will always register his or her litter; however, not *all* registered litters are from reputable breeders. An AKC registration is not a symbol of quality, but AKC show and performance titles—along with health tests—are.

puppies to aging adults—are given up to shelters and rescues across the country each year. Sadly, many of those owners relinquishing Boxers had purchased their puppies on a whim or based on emotions. Once the cuteness is gone, the Boxer is a goner.

One particularly cute fawn puppy in Tulsa, Oklahoma, purchased as an unexpected Christmas present, didn't last more than a few weeks with its new owners. By mid-January, the puppy had been banished to the backyard with only a cardboard box for its shelter against the bitterly cold weather. Fortunately, it was rescued with the help of the local Boxer rescue. The puppy suffered frostbite to its ears and other extremities and was quite ill; however, after being nurtured by its new and permanent family, it is now a healthy, happy adult.

Puppy love is a powerful force to which many dog lovers succumb. When the reality sinks in about how much work a puppy actually is, and what a lifestyle change this bundle of fur brings about, many new puppy owners' commitment wanes. Those owners who make a planned,

If you begin when your puppy is young, training can be much easier than with an adult.

educated decision to embark on raising a puppy, and who have a thorough understanding for what job lies ahead, usually do very well. Basically, raising a puppy requires the support of all family members, a good dose of commitment, a bit of creativeness to work out any potential problems, and a "do-whatever-it-takes" mind-set to make the human-dog relationship succeed.

So, before you launch into purchasing a puppy, it is critical you understand exactly what a Boxer puppy is really like. You also should be familiar with the level of care that is necessary to raise an energetic puppy, the time you will spend training the puppy in order to have a well-mannered adult, and the nec-essary financial commitment of raising a puppy; the first year can be expensive.

Good News about Puppy Ownership

Obviously, one of the greatest attractions of owning a puppy is that they are incredibly cute. They play a lot and will entertain their owners constantly with their silly and endearing antics. But, there are more good reasons for purchasing a puppy besides simply being able to enjoy the dog's once-in-a-lifetime puppy stage.

One of the most important draws to buying a Boxer puppy is that the puppy is impressionable and moldable when it is young. You, as the owner, have the ability to take this eager puppy and give it the love and training it needs to develop into a wonderful family dog and devout companion. With the correct environment, you can strongly influence the dog's adult temperament and behaviors, and help it to become a social, well-mannered pet.

Another benefit to raising a puppy is that you can influence much of the Boxer's current and future health. By scheduling regular preventive veterinary care, conducting screenings for disease at appropriate ages, and feeding a healthy, nutritious diet, an owner can help a Boxer to mature as disease-free as possible.

Also, if you want to compete with your Boxer, choosing a puppy may allow you to find a good potential prospect for your chosen sport, without paying large sums of money for a dog that is already proven in that area. For example, if you plan on showing your Boxer, you can much more affordably purchase a puppy with show potential than attempt to buy an adult dog with the same qualities. If you are looking for an obedience, agility, or Schutzhund prospect, the same is also true.

Raising a Boxer from a puppy also allows you to acclimate your dog to your lifestyle. If you have a family, rearing a puppy carefully with children and teaching it to respect little humans with unsteady gaits may be easier and safer than introducing an adult dog into the family that hasn't had experience with children and therefore is, perhaps, more

cautious or fearful of children. If you have cats or other small non-canine pets, a puppy often is more accepting of living with a cat and may or may not realize the size difference when it (the Boxer) is fully grown.

Young puppies are fairly agreeable to settle into just about any lifestyle. Do you enjoy boating? A young Boxer will be more likely to enjoy swims and rides if it is acclimated to this water life early, though it is true that old dogs *can* learn new

Temperament: Part Hereditary, Part Environment

One theory of temperament is that when a puppy is born, it will have inherited one of three possible temperaments: a steady, sound temperament, an "extreme" temperament (either aggressive or very fearful or shy), or a temperament that could develop into either a steady or an unstable one, depending on the environment the puppy is exposed to while growing up. It is also thought that the numbers of inherently "good" or "bad" puppies—those that no matter what you do will still have the temperament they were born with—is very small; therefore, the bulk of the puppies born can go either way.

So keep in mind when rearing your impressionable puppy that the environment you provide for it can make a drastic difference in the pup's behavior and temperament as it matures.

tricks. If you travel a lot, acclimating a puppy to regular road trips can be easier—and less of a cleanup—than with an adult dog.

Training can be easier, too, if you start with a young pup. With a lot of encouragement, a few yummy treats, and regular practice, a Boxer puppy often can learn the basic commands of sit, down, stay, and come by the time it is 16 weeks old. It's much easier to get a little, 12-pound (5.4-kg) Boxer pup to sit with a treat than it is to teach a boisterous, 60-plus pound (27-plus kg), untrained adult the same maneuver. Additionally, there are some activities, such as tracking and other scent work, that many trainers say are best if the puppy is introduced to the beginning stages when it is very young.

Pitfalls of Puppyhood

Puppyhood is not all fun and games, however, and there are some aspects of raising a puppy that involve a lot of time and work. In other words, it may be easier to train a Boxer when it is young and small, but you have to make the commitment to actually train the puppy. That means a one-hour class at least once a week for ten months, and daily sessions working on what you've learned, ranging in time from five minutes several times a day for little puppies, to twenty minutes or more every day for older puppies. In addition to formal training, puppy owners must be committed to acclimating their new charges to the puppy's surroundings. This means socializing the puppy with other dogs, other people, and the things that happen in the neighborhood. If you, as a Boxer owner, don't resolve yourself to carve out this time for your Boxer's training, your young, strong Boxer very quickly will be out of control and will be less than desirable as a pet.

Note: Now may be a good time to mention that lack of training is cited as the primary reason dogs are euthanized. In recent studies investigating why dogs were turned into shelters, it was found that if a dog had little or no training, it had a very high chance of being turned into the shelter. Conversely, if a dog had received training, it wasn't nearly as likely to be turned into a shelter.

This makes sense: An untrained dog is no fun to live with. The problem many owners have is that they find puppy antics "cute" and see no reason to begin the puppy's training. The puppy quickly grows into an adolescent, a full-size dog with the activity level and mind-set of a puppy. This combination spells trouble and is trying for even the most patient and understanding owner. Though the dog is still trainable at this age, many overwhelmed owners simply banish the dog to the backyard, where it barks, digs, and climbs fences. When a family member ventures out to see the dog, the person is bowled over by a tremendously excited dog. It's usually not long after this stage that the dog makes a trip to the shelter.

Don't make this mistake with your Boxer puppy. Be sure to begin early with your pup's training and stick to it. At the year's end, you'll be the one with the well-trained dog and the envy of the neighborhood.

Play: Speaking of out of control, that's how most Boxer puppies play—at high speeds and without any care about what damage they might inflict on themselves, or the things they crash into during their play. By nature, the Boxer is generally a breed with lots of energy. A well-trained adult Boxer can focus its energy on supervised play and, if given a job to perform, the adult is able to channel its energy into its work. Puppies, of course, have no job except to play, investigate, and generally look for trouble. They require constant supervision in addition to opportunities for energetic play.

Teething: All puppies go through the dreaded teething stage. At around sixteen weeks to five months, the puppy's milk teeth fall out and the adult teeth begin moving in. This physical change causes a normally chewy Boxer puppy to become a voracious one. Table legs, siding, small trees, and other objects may become the target of a teething Boxer puppy. One look at a Boxer's teeth and the strength of its bite should be an indicator of the level of destruction these babies are capable of, given a free moment.

House-training: House-training is another issue that must be addressed with puppy ownership. No puppy is perfect, and some are not as good at alerting owners to their elimination needs as others. Politely put, there are going to be accidents. Crates are going to need hosing down and carpets will need scrubbing. It's part of puppyhood. The benefit, however, is that when a pup makes a "mistake," it is less of an accident to clean than when an adult dog eliminates inappropriately.

Change in lifestyle: Then there's the abrupt change in a carefree lifestyle that a puppy brings with it. If you're used to total freedom, dashing out to join friends for the evening,

Boxer puppies are always ready to play. Regular playtime helps take the edge off their activity level and deepens the bond between owner and Boxer.

and mother, nor will it be happy to be separated from you. You'll find it amazing (perhaps distressfully so) how loudly a 10-pound (4.5-kg) puppy can yelp and howl all by itself.

Expense: Finally, as mentioned in the previous chapter, puppies can be expensive. With vaccinations, veterinary exams, ear cropping, and basic supplies, first-year expenditures can *easily* top $1,000.

So, is raising a Boxer puppy a challenge you can handle? If not, that's fine. Perhaps an adult Boxer would fit into your lifestyle better at this time. Or perhaps a Boxer just isn't realistically in the picture at all right now. That's all right, too. The important point to realize here is that if you go into puppy ownership with your eyes open and a commitment to make the relationship work no matter what happens, you will be successful.

Buying a puppy or dog from a reputable, experienced breeder greatly improves the odds of purchasing a Boxer that is healthy, looks good, and has a tremendous temperament.

taking off for a weekend getaway, or even spending the day at the beach, this will all change when you own a puppy. Your puppy will need to be fed at least three times a day. It will need to be exercised. It will need regular walks to allow it to relieve itself. A puppy can't be left in the backyard to fend for itself; it must be supervised just as you would a young child. And, don't expect to sleep much in the first few days and weeks after you bring your puppy home. Your puppy will not be happy being separated from its littermates

Finding a Breeder You Can Trust

All breeders are not created equally—nor are their dogs. In general, you get what you pay for when buying a Boxer puppy. If you want a good family Boxer, you'll need to find a good breeder. If you want a great Boxer with show or performance event potential, you'll need to seek out and work with only the most reputable breeders. This is not to say that you can't find a nice pet from another puppy source, but it's much tougher and really not a job for someone who is new to the breed.

You might ask, "Why should I pay hundreds of dollars to a breeder for a Boxer that's just going to be a pet, when I can pick one up from a newspaper ad for less than a $100?" The simple reason is that the Boxer has enough potential health problems to justify searching for one that has been bred specifically to avoid or lessen the chances of having these illnesses. If you purchase a Boxer for a small sum from a breeder who doesn't x-ray his or her dogs for hip dysplasia, or track his or her dogs for cardiomyopathy, or worry about skin allergies, you may end up paying more for the puppy's health care in its first year of life than double or triple the purchase price of a healthier, well-bred puppy. So, how can you tell if a breeder is good, great, or "other"?

The Best of the Best

Of the thousands of Boxers that are bred each year, probably only several hundred litters are from breeders with impeccable standards. These are breeders who have been actively showing and competing with their Boxers for years and even decades. Boxers are a love, a passion, and an expensive hobby for these people. Breeding Boxers is not a money-making venture for them. Top breeders have litters only when they are trying to achieve another quality Boxer for themselves, not because they're trying to make a few bucks. In fact, when a breeder takes extreme care and planning with each litter, the puppies—though perhaps more expensive than a backyard product—are not sold at a profit. Most breeders of this caliber relate that when a litter is properly planned and cared for, the puppies are sold at a loss to the breeder.

When a quality, experienced breeder has a litter, he or she has bred for soundness of conformation and health, as well as for a solid, happy Boxer temperament. If you are searching for a pet, this quality breeding is still important. In addition to being a good-looking dog, a well-bred puppy should be very robust and healthy and should have that classic, loving Boxer temperament. Breeding for these qualities takes a lot of time, research, breed knowledge, and hard work.

Breeding for Looks

Experienced breeders know the breed standard inside out and upside down, and could probably recite it verbatim with their eyes closed. They know what is considered the perfect form for a Boxer. They also understand that there has never been a Boxer without one or more deviations from the standard or flaws in either how the dog is physically put together—slope of the shoulder, shape of the eye, position of the bite—or how it moves. However, these breeders continue their efforts to work a little closer toward that "perfect" dog.

How do they do this? They track their own bloodlines and have a solid understanding of what traits or characteristics are strong (dominant) in their lines and which are weak or recessive in their lines. These breeders also know how to breed to bring out the best in their dogs, and to suppress any weak points. When they plan a breeding, these breeders will spend a great deal of time researching and considering prospective mates for their dogs. Typically, the breeder searches for a suitable stud dog for a particular female. If the breeder has selected the correct mate, the stud's traits should counter or negate the female's faults, and vice versa. The goal of the resulting

litter, therefore, should be an improvement over both parents.

Despite this careful planning, only a few pups in each litter may be recognizable, outstanding show quality. These puppies will have the potential to finish their conformation championships and, if they develop into particularly outstanding dogs, they may be able to be campaigned as "specials," competing for group and best in show wins. The remaining littermates will still be well-built, attractive Boxers. What this means to you as the pet owner is that you will have a great-looking dog with the form, function, and movement to partic-

Will this Boxer be the next champion? Experienced breeders can give you an educated guess with young puppies, but a puppy must be at least six months old before its show potential can be recognized accurately.

ipate in a wide variety of activities, both competitive and noncompetitive. The experienced breeder, as opposed to a novice or an inexperienced breeder, will be better able to determine which puppies may develop into show-quality and which will probably not. They will also be able help an owner select a puppy whose temperament meshes well with the needs of the potential owner.

Breeding for Health

The breeder whose goal is breeding quality Boxers takes the extra step to certify the health of his or her dogs *before* breeding them. Quality breeders will test their dogs for Boxer cardiomyopathy and will *not* breed a dog with this inherited disease. Breeders will also test and certify that their Boxers are free of hip dysplasia. A certification number from the Orthopedic Foundation for Animals or PennHIP should appear on the mature Boxer's pedigree. The dogs should also be certified for vision with the Canine Eye Registration Foundation (CERF) and many will have a DNA registration. The Boxers being bred should also be permanently identified, either through tattooing or microchipping (see Chapter Six). The American Kennel Club requires this permanent identification in order to record the individual health certificate registration numbers on the dog's permanent pedigree.

In addition to testing and certifying that the dogs being bred are free from inherited diseases, and thereby optimizing the probability that the ensuing puppies will be healthy, too, a good breeder also stands behind what he or she breeds.

Reputable breeders do this by offering all new puppy owners a written guarantee of their puppy's health. If the puppy has a serious health problem, the breeder will take the puppy back and will either refund the puppy owner's money or provide the person with another puppy. Also, if a puppy doesn't work out in a new owner's home *for any reason,* the reputable breeder will take that puppy back—and at any age.

Breeding for Temperament

Good breeders go beyond breeding for good looks and healthy dogs; they also breed for great temperaments. Dogs with questionable temperaments are simply not bred, even if the dog or bitch has its conformation championship. A poor temperament—aggression or severe shyness toward people—is considered a serious flaw and, given the size of the breed and the power of its bite, a quirky Boxer could inflict serious injuries. Though a bite on the ankle from a toy breed may be brushed aside and quickly forgiven, a chomp from a Boxer becomes a serious issue.

The Boxer, fortunately, is renowned for its affable, playful, even comical temperament. Though fierce looking, this breed *rarely* displays any aggression toward people unless it has been seriously mistreated or

If you have young family members, your number one criteria should be finding a puppy with a patient, steady temperament.

tured environment. You'll find that a quality breeder will be not only an excellent "dog person," but will also have the innate skills of a behaviorist and a psychiatrist, too.

The junkyard dog: Because the Boxer has a rather fierce look to those who don't know the "marshmallow" inside, there are people who will attempt to take it and twist it into something it was never intended to be—a vicious dog. They will purposely select ill-tempered, unstable dogs and breed them to dogs with similar temperaments. Their purpose, supposedly, is to develop a vicious guard dog or watchdog, or to extend their machoism by walking around with a "loaded gun on a leash."

Conversely to this philosophy, however, the best guard dogs are actually those with the *most* stable temperaments and the intelligence to know the difference between an attacker and an innocent stranger. The best guardians are also those with an intense desire to please their owners and obey their commands, even in unlikely circumstances.

Because of a few bad apples, however, Boxer owners should make sure they are model dog owners to prevent the potential of a city or state proposing a breed ban law that includes Boxers.

What You Can Expect from a Breeder

In addition to a scrupulously planned breeding program, really good breeders are very careful

poorly bred. With this in mind, the reputable breeder does not even consider breeding a Boxer unless it has the true Boxer temperament and is steady and trusting with people.

What this relates to is that instead of worrying if a puppy has the potential to be aggressive toward people or not, a puppy owner can focus his or her concerns on choosing the Boxer pup that has the best personality to fit his or her lifestyle. Experienced breeders know what temperaments work well with active individuals, what traits are good for families with small children, and what pups will fit into a more struc-

about the homes in which their puppies are placed. If you plan on purchasing a puppy from a quality breeder, you can expect to be questioned, in a friendly way, of course, about your lifestyle, your living arrangements, and your plans for the puppy, as well as whether you have the full support of your family members, if you have family. If you work during the day, the breeder will want to know who will be able to walk and feed the puppy when you're not around. The breeder will also want to know if you have a fenced backyard and whether you plan on making this dog an indoor dog or an outdoor dog. (The correct answer is an indoor dog with lots of supervised, outdoor playtime!)

In addition, a reputable breeder will most likely want you to come to his or her home and have your entire family meet some adult Boxers. The reason for this is for the breeder to meet you in person, and for you and your family to meet a group of nicely behaved adult Boxers. The key word here is "adult." Many times, dog lovers fall in love with the puppy without taking into consideration just how big and strong and jubilant an adult Boxer can be. Also, sometimes small children, though they are familiar with dogs and comfortable around smaller breeds, are intimidated or frightened by the Boxer's size. Additionally, an uncertain spouse may go the other way when he or she meets a Boxer "up close." The breeder knows that these potential conflicts are better addressed directly and resolved amicably before an exuberant puppy enters the picture.

Please don't be put off by the inquisitiveness or the "pre-reqs" of these breeders; they're not trying to be nosy or pushy, they're just trying to be sure that their puppies go to

Quality breeders know what it takes to raise a Boxer pup successfully.

Who can resist this face? You can if a puppy is not the right option for you at this time.

people who are going to be able to properly care for and raise the puppy. Reputable breeders know what it takes to raise a Boxer puppy and they are acutely aware of why Boxers fail in certain homes. They want to make sure that the recipients of their puppies are well equipped and ready to take on this job.

Champion Bloodlines

Beware of want ads advertising "Champion Bloodlines." A large percentage of Boxer pedigrees will have a token champion many generations back—which means literally nothing. Parents and grandparents that are champions *are* champion bloodlines.

An added bonus of purchasing a puppy from a breeder who really knows what he or she is doing with the breed is that you will have a support network for life. You will be able to call this breeder with any question or problem and either be able to get a good answer and sound advice toward solving your Boxer problem, or the breeder will know where and how to get the answer to your question. These folks have a wealth of information and enough cannot be said about how much support good breeders give to all of their puppy owners. For this great relationship to develop, however, you must be comfortable talking with and consulting the breeder. If you have the impression that the breeder might think you're being tedious or may tire of your questions, you might consider another breeder. All of the breeder's vast experience is no help to you if you aren't comfortable communicating with him or her.

Beware When You Buy

Of the thousands of Boxers that are bred each year, it is safe to say that less than 25 percent are products of reputable breeders. The majority of registered, and unregistered, Boxer puppies are the result of what are called "backyard" breedings. These breeders, though perhaps well intentioned, do not show their dogs nor do they compete in performance events. They haven't screened or certified their dogs for hereditary diseases, nor have they studied the genetic tendencies of certain hereditary traits. In most cases, they have a well-loved female Boxer and they want to have a puppy "just like her." The rest of the litter they figure they will sell to friends and neighbors, maybe advertise in the local newspaper, and perhaps even make a little profit.

You may be able to find a nice Boxer puppy from a neighborhood litter and the puppy will undoubtedly cost less than a puppy from a reputable breeder. Your chances of purchasing a puppy with health problems, however, are far greater with the backyard breeder than with one who has done his or her homework, has verified the health of the parents, and guarantees the puppies' health. Also, the backyard Boxer puppy is not the pup you'd want to purchase if you are considering competing in conformation; there won't be any show-quality puppies here. It also may not have the form or temperament needed to compete in many performance events.

Another important consideration is that since the backyard breeder is inexperienced, puppy owners will not be able to turn to this individual for advice and problem solving. And, because backyard breeders have no facilities to keep any dogs other than their own, they will not be able to— nor will they express a desire to— take back your puppy for whatever reason.

Again, this is *not* to say that a nice family pet Boxer can't be found from a source such as this. It just means that if you buy a puppy from an inex-

perienced breeder, it is a buyer-beware sort of purchase. You may be able to select the pet of your dreams that lives a healthy and full life free of health problems. Or you could wind up with a puppy that has inherited every possible ailment known to dogdom and quickly rack up veterinary bills that far exceed the price of what you would have paid for a well-bred, health-guaranteed Boxer.

But, there are worse sources for Boxers. There are Boxer breeders— and this term is used loosely—who use their dogs for profit only, period. Their goal is simply to produce puppies as a cash crop. Corners are cut, vaccinations are skipped, and little concern or thought is given to what dog is being bred to what dog and how that breeding might affect the outcome of the health, temperaments, and conformation of the puppies. Also, the dogs and puppies are kept in substandard condition and have little if any positive interaction with people. These breeders then sell their puppies to puppy brokers who distribute the puppies to sellers around the country. Many of these puppies end up for sale in pet stores.

Though these puppies have been bred and raised in poor conditions, this is, again, not to say that you can't find a nice pet from this source. It's just that the cards are stacked against you for finding a puppy that is healthy in mind and body. Also, if you purchase a puppy from this source, you are supporting the puppy farmers' business. Not a very nice thought, is it?

How to Find That Great Breeder

Now that you know why you want to go to a really good, experienced breeder for your Boxer puppy, how exactly do you find this person? This is the hardest part. These breeders don't advertise their litters in local newspapers. If they do advertise their litters, beyond simply word of mouth, it is generally in publications, such as the breed magazine, the *Boxer Review,* or perhaps on the breeder's personal web page. Despite the lack of publicity, these breeders often have their puppies sold even before they are born. Because of the reputation that precedes some breeders, there are those breeders who actually will have show, performance, and pet owners literally lining up for the expected puppies. In order to be sure of receiving a puppy from a litter, puppy owners are often required to make a deposit to reserve an unborn puppy.

Boxer rescue: At first glance, this doesn't seem to be a source for breeders; after all, these folks are rescuing unwanted Boxers, right? Yes, but did you know this group rescues puppies, too? If you don't want to adopt a Boxer puppy, these folks can still help. The American Boxer Rescue Association (ABRA) can be one of the very best places to ask for a quality breeder referral, since these rescue folks *know* which breeders take their dogs back and which don't. They also know who stands behind their breedings and provides positive support for their puppy owners. If you need to go out of your area to find a truly great breeder, your local rescue workers will be very frank with you and won't hedge corners. If you want a puppy, ABRA wants to make sure you are directed toward a breeder who, in turn, will make sure you go into the endeavor with your eyes open and your feet well planted on the ground. Enough said. These people are tops. For phone numbers, web sites, and e-mail addresses, see Useful Addresses and Literature, page 196.

United States Boxer Association: This national club focuses on the European and German ideal of the Boxer as a working and structurally correct dog. Members are active in agility, obedience, tracking, scent work (drug dogs), and Schutzhund competitions. The club also offers ZTP tests and European-style conformation shows. If you are looking for a Boxer with the intention of competing in performance events, a call to this organization would be able to direct you to a list of more specialized Boxer breeders. For phone numbers, web sites, and e-mail addresses, see Useful Addresses and Literature, page 195.

Dog shows: If you want to meet several breeders at a time and see a sampling of their dogs, attend a dog show in your area. You'll find a lot of breeders and owners sitting ringside before, during, and after the judging. This is a great opportunity to meet some fine Boxer people in your area, make some important contacts, and learn a lot about the breed. You'll also quickly find out who has puppies or upcoming litters. Be forewarned, however, that there are some breeders and owners who are rather intense and a bit nervous when their dogs are being judged and prefer not to talk during this time; unfortunately, they don't wear signs that say, "Leave me alone! My dog is in the ring." After the judging is over, most anyone is easily approachable.

Another great place to meet and talk with Boxer owners at a dog show is far away from the excitement of the show ring. It's a place many lovingly refer to as the "RV Camp." This is where dog owners and handlers stay with their dogs during the day while waiting for their next event. Other than the time just prior to ring time, the atmosphere here is very laid back and quite congenial. You will find that most owners here will be more than happy to talk to you about Boxers in general and their own dogs. A stroll through this area can be even more fun than watching the judging.

Local breed club: No show in your area anytime soon? Check with the ABC to see if there is a local Boxer club near you. If there is, you can call the contact person for this club—usually the secretary—and see if this person can direct you to a reputable breeder in your area. The names, locations, and contact information for ABC-member clubs can easily be found on the ABC web site, too (see Useful Addresses and Literature, page 195).

A puppy is an investment: You will receive tenfold what you put into this relationship.

All-breed dog clubs: In many areas, there may not be a local Boxer club, but there may be an all-breed club. Find out who the corresponding secretary is for this club and see if he or she can refer you to a few reputable Boxer members. These members may not be breeders themselves, but they may be able to point you in the right direction toward a top breeder.

Veterinarian: If you know a good veterinarian in your area, he or she could be a very good source for information about breeders. At the very least, your veterinarian will know which ones take good care of their Boxers and breed quality dogs. If you have a veterinarian, ask him or her to recommend a breeder.

Obedience clubs: If you have a training club near you, ask one of the trainers if he or she can make any recommendations for Boxer breeders. Good breeders strongly advocate obedience training Boxers, so if there's a reputable breeder in your area, the trainers in this club should be familiar with the individual.

Advertisements: Be wary of this source. Anyone can place a slick, color advertisement in a magazine but that doesn't mean they are reputable breeders. Magazines have no criteria for breeders to meet other than that the check for the ad space clears the bank. Some publications are better sources for dog breeders than others, and, as mentioned previously, the breed magazine, *Boxer Review,* is probably the best known. Since this publication is geared toward show breeders, it reaches few pet owners, and advertisers are not trying to reach the mass puppy market. If looking in general interest dog magazines, be sure to read between the lines of the advertisements. If the ad touts "puppies all the time," avoid this breeder! If the ad is *not* promoting championship bloodlines and dogs that are tested (and certified "clear") for hereditary diseases, be sure to question this aspect, if you call.

Finding a Puppy That's Best for You

Now you're at the fun point. You've found the breeder you want to work with and that breeder has a litter coming up. What do you do now? If you walk into the breeder's home and are faced with as many as six or more wriggly, bouncy Boxer

When you buy your puppy, you are solely responsible for its outcome in life. Make sure you raise your Boxer to its full, loving potential.

puppies, how will you decide which one to take home? And, will your decision be the best one?

General Impressions

Take a look at the overall condition of the breeder's facility. Have the puppies been raised in the home? Have they been raised in a modern and clean kennel? Or are they in filthy conditions, exposed to the elements in the backyard or in a decaying barn? If you are looking for a puppy to be with your family, the puppy should come from a clean and loving environment. The breeder should already have made a concerted effort to expose the puppy to all facets of everyday life. If for any reason you are unhappy or uncomfortable with the premises or the overall condition of the dogs and puppies, leave immediately *without* a puppy. Your gut instincts will *not* lead you astray in this situation. Poor conditions indicate an irresponsible breeder.

Pick Your Purpose

One way to narrow the field is to decide ahead of time if there is a particular role you want your Boxer to fill. Do you want to get involved in dog shows? Compete in agility? Or, are you just looking for a great pet? Deciding what you want can help you and your breeder select that perfect puppy.

Show: If you are interested in entering the competitive world of dog showing, you must find a puppy with wonderful conformation and enough flash to be noticed by the judges. The puppy must also be a great mover, and possess that classic, irresistible Boxer temperament. Though many puppies in a well-bred litter may do reasonably well in the show ring and can pick up a few ribbons and perhaps a few points toward their championship, there are few puppies in the litter that will have what it takes to do very well in the show ring and finish a championship. Among these elite Boxers, there are even fewer that will be able to rack up multiple breed wins, group placements, maybe even a Best in Show.

Knowing which puppy in a litter shows the promise of being a future champion or more, is a mixture of skill, knowledge of the breed, and gut instinct. Many puppies that look terrific at 12 or 16 weeks do not turn out as expected. For this reason, a show-quality puppy is generally not sold until it is four or five months old (or older), when the breeder has a better feel for how the puppy will develop. Other puppies that look good but aren't considered "pick of the litter," have been known to develop beyond an owner's wildest dreams and succeed in the show ring.

A show-quality puppy is not a guarantee of a magnificent dog; it is the breeder's educated guess based on what the puppy looks like at an early age. The show-quality puppy may cost a bit more than the other puppies in the litter, but it is the only way to go if you plan on showing. Because there will be very few puppies in the litter that are show quality, you will have very few pups to pick from. In fact, you may simply be asked: "Male or female?" Or, maybe there won't even be a choice.

Note: Americans like their Boxers flashy, but this doesn't mean that a plain Boxer can't win, too. Flashy dogs, with white markings on their legs, chest, and collar, have traditionally been favored over solid fawn or brindle Boxers. In recent years, however, plain Boxers have been winning more and more. So a Boxer that has tremendous conformation, temperament, and movement should be competitive in the future even with few or no white markings. Also, when selecting a show-quality puppy, the breeder may ask to co-own the pup with you. Usually, this means that the breeder will have input into the dog's show career and will be able to select puppies from future litters if the puppy is a female, or be allowed stud service if the puppy is a male. Depending on the breeder, co-ownership may also be a great benefit for the novice owner and his or her first show puppy because the breeder can provide much needed guidance and expertise in raising, showing, and breeding your Boxer. However, if you do not fully understand what is involved in co-ownership, or if you are not willing to abide by the terms, then it is best to avoid it.

Performance/working: If you are looking for a Boxer that will be able to participate in performance events, you need to relay this information to your breeder, too. An experienced breeder can help direct you toward Boxers with temperaments that are most suitable for sports, such as a puppy that is eager to please, looks for human direction, and enjoys close companionship. The puppy will also need to possess a certain amount of athleticism and drive.

Companion: Though every Boxer in a well-bred litter should make a good pet, if you are interested only in having a great canine partner, then you don't need to consider its show prospects. This puppy, though good-looking and bred for health and a good temperament, may not quite have what it takes to compete in the show ring. The flaw may be minor, and virtually unnoticed by anyone other than a serious Boxer breeder or judge, but it is usually enough to classify the puppy as "pet" or "companion" quality. The puppy's flaws are also those that make it unsuitable to be bred.

With a pet-quality dog, you can expect the breeder to require that you sign a spay/neuter registration. Or the breeder may only provide you with a Limited Registration (see page 61), which means you can participate in many performance events, but cannot compete in the show ring. You will also be required to supply proof of spay/neuter to receive your registration.

Male or Female?

Many people mistakenly say, "I want a female," because they think a female dog is the sweeter of the sexes. With Boxers, this is not nec-

Are you interested in performance events? Be sure to discuss this with your breeder to help you select the best puppy for your purposes.

essarily true. Some of the best snugglers and Boxers with the easiest-going temperaments can be males. If you're looking for the best temperament, don't limit yourself to one sex or the other; much like people, each Boxer has its own unique personality. If you already own a dog, however, and you want to introduce the Boxer puppy as the second pet, then you may want to carefully consider which sex puppy you choose.

As a general rule, fewer troubles tend to erupt with paired dogs of the opposite sexes. For example, if you already own a male dog, you will want to look for a compatible female. If your dog at home is a dominant type, you will also want to consider a less "alpha" temperament in the puppy. Boxers generally get along relatively well with each other, but many Boxer owners say that once a Boxer dislikes another dog, the grudge is forever.

Color

One thing the Boxer doesn't lack is color; brindles and fawns come in nearly every shade and hue imaginable. Some Boxers are "flashy" and have a lot of white markings; others are plain and have little if any white. Still others are pure white or "check," with spots of fawn or brindle. If you are looking for a show-quality Boxer, color and markings may not be as critical as in past years. Judges are now being encouraged to judge plain Boxers on equal terms with flashy dogs. If you are looking for a companion dog or one to compete in performance events, any color goes. A word to the wise, however: With a companion dog, don't rule out a puppy with a great temperament if it is in a color other than your first choice.

Cropped and Docked, or Au Naturel?

Many breeders in the United States automatically have their veterinarians dock their puppies' tails and remove dewclaws shortly after being whelped, and crop ears between 9 and 12 weeks of age. If you do not want your puppy cropped and/or docked, you will need to discuss this issue with your breeder. Chances are that you will not be able to purchase an undocked puppy, simply because this procedure is done when the puppy is newly whelped. However, there may be room to negotiate with the Boxer's ears.

Alternatively, if you want to have your Boxer's ears cropped, make sure you consult with your breeder about which veterinarian to use for this procedure. The long show crops can be quite tricky and if not properly cut and given appropriate aftercare for weeks and even months following the surgery, the ears may not stand up properly. To avoid a flop, literally, make sure you have the procedure done properly and make sure your Boxer puppy is in skilled and respected hands.

When You Meet the Puppies

Enjoy the moment. Hold the puppies. Play with them. Bask in the experience of being able to take part in puppy play without all the worries of puppy care on a large scale. It won't take long when visiting a group of pups before their individual temperaments begin to emerge and become apparent. Once you've gotten a bit of puppy play out of your system, you'll need to begin buckling down to the business of deciding which Boxer puppy will be the one for you.

An experienced breeder will be extremely helpful in helping you sort through the temperaments, conformation, and overall potential of the puppies, the more you know about this selection, the more assured you will be that you've selected the right puppy.

Temperament Testing

There are two temperaments that you'll want to avoid, if possible, in selecting your puppy:

1. The first temperament to avoid is the fearful puppy. An experienced Boxer owner who has a lot of time and patience may be able to take this puppy and calm its fears. A fearful puppy probably would not make a good companion for the novice or inexperienced Boxer owner.

Note: An entire litter of fearful puppies indicates that the dogs have not been properly socialized by the breeder. These pups are best avoided since their mental condition shows a lack of concern from the breeder.

2. The second temperament that should be avoided by a novice or first-time Boxer owner is the very bold puppy that enjoys bossing his or her littermates around. This puppy could be showing some dominance aggression tendencies that, though not insurmountable with appropriate socialization and training, could be a bit more than many pet owners would want to deal with. In other words, this puppy may, at maturity, try to exert its dominance over family members.

In most litters, the "middle" puppies are usually the best temperament choices. They are happy, playful, not shy, and not too bold, either. This also is the group in which there is the greatest number of puppies from which to choose. From this group you'll want to find the puppy that enjoys being picked up without excessive wiggling, comes when you've got its attention, and likes to follow people when they walk by. All of these traits help to indicate a puppy that will enjoy human contact and will be an eager student in training sessions.

If you want a Boxer to grow up with natural ears, be sure to advise your breeder of this before you purchase your puppy.

Physical Examining

When looking at a litter of puppies, it is important to physically handle them and look for signs of good health.

• The puppy's coat should be smooth and clean without any missing patches, which might indicate ringworm, mange, or a variety of unwanted skin conditions.

• Check the puppy for fleas and ticks; it should have neither.

• How does the skin look? Is it smooth, or is it bumpy or flaky and dry? Can you find any pustules, which might indicate an allergy or former flea or tick bites? Again, any deviation from the norm can be an indicator of ill health.

• Do the puppy's eyes look bright? Or are they weeping?

• What about the puppy's orifices? If you detect a discharge from any of these areas, this could indicate that the puppy is ill. If you happen to see the puppy relieve itself, diarrhea and/or blood in the stool is a red flag for worms, parvovirus, or giardia.

• Also, look at the puppy when it stands and when it is moving about. Does it appear to be symmetrical with legs of equal length? Does it move freely? If you are selecting a show dog, you'll need to pay particular attention not only to how the dog is put together, but also to how it moves. A great-moving Boxer commands attention.

Making the Selection

So many puppies, so little time! Though the task of choosing a Boxer puppy can be a tough one, the stress of making a decision can be reduced if you do your research and are prepared to make a decision by using some common sense. Usually, after a session with the puppies, there is one particular pup that catches your eye and your heart. (If one puppy does not stand out, come back later for a second look.) If this puppy has a great temperament, is put together well, and comes from a good breeder with a track record of healthy dogs, you should feel comfortable in your selection.

Note: Never take your children with you to select a puppy. The begging and pleading of children may pressure you to purchase a puppy that is not best for your family. Make the selection first and either bring the puppy home or bring your children back at a later time to pick up the new family member.

Now it's time to enjoy. When you take this puppy home, you "become" its mother, its littermates, and its breeder. You are the one it will look up to for all its needs and guidance. Take this responsibility seriously and your Boxer is sure to reward you with the best it can give you.

Chapter Five

Adopting the Adult Boxer

For those who find rearing a perpetual motion Boxer puppy a little daunting, or for those dog lovers who are interested in "doing the right thing," adopting an adult dog might be just the ticket. Or, maybe you're someone who wants to know exactly what you're getting before you buy it. These and many other reasons are given in favor of the argument for adopting an adult Boxer. If adopting from a Boxer rescue, you can be assured that the Boxer experts will match you with the best adult Boxer possible. However, be aware that most municipal pounds and many nonprofit shelters do not have the resources to provide extensive temperament testing and screening. If adopting a Boxer from one of these sources, it is highly recommended that you take an experienced Boxer owner with you to evaluate the dog, transport the dog in a crate immediately to your veterinarian for an additional evaluation, and then take the Boxer home, after it has been bathed, dipped, groomed, vaccinated, and spayed or neutered.

Benefits and Drawbacks

Yes, it's true: With an adult Boxer you miss the cute cuddly months. But you also miss the teething, chewing, house-training, crate-training, and many other aspects of puppy ownership. Of course, adopting an adult Boxer is not without its challenges, too. Most adult dog adopters, however, say that the benefits far outweigh the challenges, and relate that the experience is so fulfilling that they'll never go the puppy route again.

Note: It is estimated that 25 percent or more of all dogs in shelters are purebreds. Shelter workers relate that purebred dogs are often hard to place because they are viewed suspiciously by potential adopters. People tend to accept mixed breeds in shelters, but think that if a purebred is in the shelter, it must have done something really bad to be there. Not so, say shelter and rescue workers. Most purebreds in shelters were impulse purchases as puppies by people who lacked either the ability

Boxers often end up at shelters and in Boxer Rescue because their owners did not fully realize the time and finances required to raise a puppy.

or the commitment to properly raise and care for the dog.

As one of the most popular breeds in the United States, Boxers make up a large share of these unwanted pets. Boxer Rescue estimates that thousands of Boxers are relinquished each year. Although Boxer Rescue itself places thousands of Boxers annually, many slip through the cracks.

Knowing What You Have

With an adult Boxer, what you see is what you get. There'll be no guessing as to whether that cropped ear will or won't flop over. Hoping that those slightly cowed hocks will straighten up is a moot point with an adult: Either they're straight by now, or not. When you adopt an adult, you'll know exactly how your Boxer will look when it's an adult, because it is an adult.

With an adult dog, you will have the ability to know what types of diseases it may or may not have inherited before you commit your heart to owning the dog. Mature dogs can be tested for some heart problems, degenerative spinal diseases, deafness, vision problems, and hip and elbow dysplasia. Other health problems that often go undetected in younger puppies, such as skin problems, allergies, and epilepsy, already should be evident in the adult dog. Instead of playing a wait-and-see

Indefinite Listing Privilege (ILP)

You've adopted a purebred Boxer and you want to compete in some of the AKC's performance events, but your rescued Boxer doesn't have any registration papers. In other words, you have no proof that your Boxer is a purebred. What do you do?

Apply for an Indefinite Listing Privilege (ILP) number from the AKC. With this number, your Boxer will be able to participate in most AKC events, such as agility, tracking, and obedience. (Conformation classes are off limits to ILP dogs.)

In order to receive an ILP number, the Boxer owner must fill out an application form, provide clear side, front, and back photos of the dog, and supply proof of spaying or neutering. A check must also accompany the application. Call the AKC to find out the amount. The AKC reviews the photos and the application form, confirms that the dog looks like a purebred Boxer, and then issues an ILP number. This number is good for most competitions for the life of the dog.

For more information on how to apply for an ILP number, call the AKC at (919) 233-9767, or visit the following web page: *http://www. akc.org/ILP.*

game with a puppy, with an adult dog you'll have the ability to find out whether it has any serious health problems.

In addition to knowing how your adult Boxer looks and being able to screen for many serious diseases, you will also be able to determine the dog's temperament and its activity level. If you are looking for a Boxer that is a bit calmer and less active, you may be able to find this combination with an older adult Boxer. If you went with a puppy, you may have to wait eight years before your Boxer is "less active."

When you adopt an adult dog, you'll also be able to tell whether this dog has developed into a canine with the abilities and aptitude for any sports you might be interested in

competing in. Granted, it may take you much longer to find a Boxer that can compete in agility or obedience work, but adopting an adult dog takes the guesswork out of how trainable your Boxer will be when it hits adolescence or maturity.

Avoiding Puppy Problems

Chewing: Another advantage to adopting an adult dog is that a mature dog has already passed the teething stage. This is not to say that your adult Boxer won't love to chew, or that it won't destroy a piano leg given a chance. It just means that as an adult, your Boxer won't go through a period of the awful, insatiable desire to gnaw on everything in sight as its adult teeth erupt. With appropriate toys and supervised activities, an adult Boxer may have significantly fewer problems with chewing than a teething puppy on a toothy, seek-and-destroy mission.

House-training: Still another puppy challenge that can be avoided when adopting a mature Boxer is house-training. With puppies, there will always be at least a few accidents before the puppy gains control of its bodily functions, starting around four months for consistent control. With an adult Boxer, the bodily control situation is already covered, and, many rescued Boxers already know to do their duties outside; in some cases, no house-training is needed at all. Imagine that! For some owners, that benefit is worth the ticket right there. Adult dogs that aren't formerly house-trained can be quickly trained using a crate and careful supervision. As one adopted dog owner exclaimed, "It took *months* to house-train the puppy, and two days to train the adult."

Speaking of training, old dogs *do* learn new tricks. The desire to please its owner does not diminish with age. Adult boxers are eager learners. Because of their age and maturity, they are more focused and can concentrate for longer periods of time, making training sessions go much faster. Remember, half the battle with training a puppy is simply getting the pup's attention for more than a nanosecond. With lots of positive reinforcement and a few yummy treats, even a Boxer that is untrained and is considered a "handful" can quickly be roped in and developed into a model citizen.

Challenges of the Adopted Boxer

It would not be fair to say that adopting an adult dog is *not* without its challenges. In many cases, the adult Boxer transitions quickly into its new home and becomes a beloved pet, but in other cases, a more experienced owner may be needed to help "undo" some of the damage done by the previous owner, and the transitioning from rescued Boxer to family Boxer takes some creativity, patience, and time.

Rescued Boxers are screened for health problems and are thoroughly evaluated for temperament.

Old dogs do learn new tricks, and many rescued Boxers have the ability to compete in performance events.

Not Knowing

Perhaps the biggest challenge in adopting a rescued Boxer is "not knowing"—not knowing how the Boxer was raised as a puppy, or what types of things it is quirky about. For example, one rescued Boxer suffered from severe separation anxiety. The owner discovered this fact when he left the Boxer unattended while he walked to the mailbox. When he returned a few moments later, the Boxer had torn the drapes and blinds off the window facing the mailbox. Another Boxer had a former gunshot injury that no one knew about until the dog was touched in the "hot" or formerly tender spot. The dog didn't bite, but she let out a yelp that startled everyone.

Fortunately, if a Boxer is placed through a branch of the ABRA, it has been thoroughly examined and temperament tested by both an experienced Boxer breeder/owner and/or a veterinarian. The Boxer is fostered by a member of the breed rescue program to further determine if the dog has any fears, quirks, or oddities that might catch an owner by surprise. When the Boxer is fully assessed, it is then considered ready for adoption.

Health Headaches and Heartaches

Adopting an adult Boxer can be an expensive veterinary adventure. When a Boxer is unwanted enough that its owners are willing to drop it off at a shelter, the dog frequently has been medically or socially neglected and, in rare cases, physically abused. Many rescued Boxers come from homes where they were poorly fed and are very thin. Their coats are so brittle from malnutrition that it literally falls out as they walk. It can take months to bring a dog back from this condition, and even longer before it regains healthy skin and a glossy coat.

Some rescued Boxers have received little if any veterinary attention. Most need worming. Some have flea infestations that are so severe the dogs are deathly ill when they enter the rescue program. Heartworm is rampant in many areas of the country, and untreated Boxers in these areas are almost always infected.

Some Boxers walk into their new homes and immediately settle in as if they've lived there all their lives. Others take a bit longer to adjust, but with love, patience, and training, a rescued Boxer makes a tremendous pet.

Depending on the age and health of the dog and the degree of the infestation, the Boxer may or may not be treatable.

All of these conditions can create some rather costly veterinary bills and require extensive attention and care from the owner. For the most part, however, if the Boxer comes from a rescue organization where the dog is screened and treated for health problems, the adoptive owner is aware of the dog's condition prior to adopting it. Many times, the rescue has already provided for the dog's veterinary care and has covered this cost, too. So, even in cases in which it may be very expensive to bring the dog back into good shape, the owner enters into this canine venture completely aware of the situation.

Bigger Issues

When a fully grown dog relieves itself inappropriately in the house, it's a bigger accident to clean up than that of a small puppy. (Crate-training is still a must with adults!) And, when a 60-pound (27-kg) Boxer decides to chew, instead of finding a puppy-size mess, such as a shredded pillow, you may come home to find the whole couch ripped apart.

Training an untrained, adult Boxer can be a bigger issue than working with a small, wriggly puppy, too. Training a stubborn, strong dog can quickly turn the "walking nicely on a leash" exercise into an arm socket-wrenching drag around the block.

Though many well-bred Boxers do end up in rescue, the majority are pet quality, which does not affect their ability to love their owners.

Fortunately, however, there are solutions to all these problems and with a little patience, ingenuity, and determination, there is hardly a problem that can't be overcome in time.

Adult Dog Sources

Just as the quality of a puppy can vary greatly with the quality of the breeder, the quality of the adult dog adoption depends on the organization handling the adoptions. In other words, there are many sources for great adult Boxers. The success of the placement, however, depends largely on the evaluation skills of the

"rescuer" and the policies of the organization regarding adoption.

Boxer Rescue

The most highly organized rescue network for Boxers is the ABRA. Founded in 1982 by Boxer breeder Tracy Hendrickson of Tulsa, Oklahoma, as an independent rescue, the ABC pledged its financial and membership support in 1989. Today, ABRA is comprised of a national network of experienced Boxer breeders, owners, and admirers of the breed who are willing to devote their time and energies to rescuing Boxers. ABRA has representatives in nearly every state who actively rescue Boxers of all ages.

The reason that Boxer Rescue is such a tremendous source for adult dogs is because of the thorough job these people perform when placing a Boxer, and because of the network members' vast experience with Boxers. These people live, breathe, and know Boxers. They can quickly judge a dog's temperament and know exactly what type of owner and what kind of home would best suit the dog.

Every dog is thoroughly evaluated for temperament and health, spayed or neutered, and treated for any health problems *before* being placed in a new home. Many dogs are fostered with volunteers who not only help nurse the dogs back to health, if necessary, but also work with the dogs on basic life skills, such as simple commands and house-training. With few exceptions, no Boxers are placed into permanent homes until they are considered to be good companions and, if they've been ill, are recovered, or are well on their way to recovery.

This organization even finds "special" homes for "special" Boxers. For example, rescuers say that older Boxers that have a few minor medical problems and perhaps an ache or pain here or there are often placed with older humans who appreciate the gentleness of these older Boxers and can relate to having to take a few meds for various minor conditions. Boxer Rescue also has puppies from time to time that are available for adoption.

If you can't adopt an adult Boxer, there are still many ways you can support Boxer Rescue.

1. Foster homes: People are always needed to temporarily house rescued Boxers.

2. "In-kind" donations: Contact your local rescue to find out what kinds of supplies are needed such as food, collars, leashes, blankets, or crates.

3. Cash donations: These are always appreciated.

4. Other special skills: Newsletter writers, photographers, and those who can help transport Boxers from shelters to veterinary offices are just a few of the volunteer services that may be needed, and appreciated, in your area.

Adopting from Boxer Rescue: What to Expect

With Boxer Rescue's breed experience, the group knows what Boxers will do well in which environments and with what type of owner. And, with the national network of rescues in place and operating, a prospective Boxer adopter should be able to find a representative in their immediate area or at least within an easy driving distance.

Because Boxer Rescue operates a bit differently from a typical pound or a nonprofit shelter without the facilities for extensive services, it bears mentioning how Boxer Rescue works and to explain the steps a prospective Boxer adopter will need to take. Though the process may seem a bit involved, it all runs fairly smoothly. Rescuers remind us, too, that this careful process is necessary to find good, permanent homes for the rescued Boxers.

Application/screening: The first stage in adopting a Boxer is filling out an application form. Many times this form is mailed to you after requesting information on the rescue program. Occasionally, you may have the opportunity to fill out an application in person if the rescue people are at a pet fair.

The application is usually divided into two sections: personal background information and what you are looking for in a Boxer. The personal background information the rescue will want to know is your address and phone number, who lives with you and their ages, what your experience has been with dogs and other pets, what types of pets you own now, how you intend to keep your Boxer—indoors, outdoors (wrong answer), or both—and why you are interested in adopting a Boxer.

The second half of the questionnaire deals with the specifics of what qualities you are looking for in your next Boxer, such as, the color, male or female, age range, AKC registered or not, and any special abilities (such as the ability to perform in agility, obedience, or Schutzhund).

When you're filling out this application, do yourself, the rescue, and the potential Boxer a favor—be honest! Don't answer falsely just because you think your true answer is not the one the rescue wants to hear. Rescues want their Boxers to go to good homes, but they also know there are no perfect owners nor are there perfect homes. These rescues are looking for people who are willing to make changes, if necessary, to their homes and yards and alter their lifestyles in order to satisfy the needs of the dogs. For every potential sticking point, there is a viable solution, if the owner is willing to be a little flexible. So, be honest. Your sincerity not only will gain you the trust of the rescuer, it will also help the rescue to pair you with the best Boxer match possible.

Once you've mailed in your application, you will receive a phone call from the rescue. It is perfectly OK to call them to confirm that they received your application. These folks can get very busy with rescues and they wouldn't be human if a form or letter was temporarily buried on a desk or counter for a few days.

When the rescue calls, it will be for an informal interview. The rescuer may have a few questions regarding how you answered some questions. For example, if you said your yard wasn't fenced, the rescue may want to know when you plan on putting up your fence. Or if you have a fence, the rescue may want to know what type of fence you have and how tall it is. You can expect more detailed questioning on your previous pets and even how they died. (Don't expect an overly warm response if you've owned three dogs in two years and they were all hit by cars.) If you have children, the rescuer will want to know their ages, their attitudes toward animals, and if they've had any experience with dogs.

If all goes well here you will either be approved and put on the waiting list for a suitable Boxer, or you may be asked if a representative of the rescue organization can come by for a home visit.

Home visit: A home visit doesn't necessarily mean that the Boxer Rescue doesn't trust your answers. If they thought you were a "front" for a research laboratory, you wouldn't have even gotten this far. Many rescues visit the applicant's home as a matter of course. It allows them to meet the prospective owner and family where they are most comfortable—in their own home. It also allows them to see any potential problems and suggest solutions to rectify the situation.

The rescue visitor often brings a Boxer with him or her for the family to meet. If the adopter is not single and has a spouse and/or children, it is important for the rescue organization to see the support of the dog adoption made by every family member. As is true of many things, the dog adoption is only as strong as its weakest link. If you have a spouse who is lukewarm about adopting a Boxer, the spouse's apprehensions need to be addressed immediately and resolved *before the Boxer is adopted.* The rescue coordinator's experience and advice can help calm many trepidations and provide reasonable solutions for some concerns; however, the final balancing act is within the family.

Waiting list: You've come a long way, and now you've got to wait. Adopting a dog is not like purchasing a puppy where you know when the litter will be available and can select the exact date on which you bring your puppy home. With dog adoption, it's a wait-and-see option. You wait while the rescue sees if it has a Boxer that will suit you well. Depending on your lifestyle and other factors, Boxer Rescue may have the "right" Boxer in as little as a day or two, or it may be a month or more. Since the rescue has no way of knowing what Boxer it will be rehoming next, it's often impossible to guess just how long your wait will be. Remember: The waiting list is not first come, first served. Each dog is matched with the person that the rescue thinks is best for that dog. If you are the type of person who could do well with a wide range of Boxers, have a home that can immediately accommodate a dog, are experienced training dogs, and aren't picky about the color or sex of the dog, you will probably be called before the harder-to-fit applicants on the list.

Rest assured that when Boxer Rescue gets in a dog it thinks might be a good match, you *will* get a phone call. You will be asked to come visit the dog at its foster home. Often, the matches are right on and it's love at first sight. However, if the dog isn't what you expected, tell the rescue. If you're somewhere in between—for instance, you wanted a fawn female and this is a brindle male—the rescue may suggest you take the dog home for the weekend and see how you feel. By Sunday afternoon, you may find that rescue knows best and you wouldn't part with your Boxer for the world. On the other hand, the weekend visit may confirm your concerns about a particular dog.

The key to a good match is keeping an open mind toward the adult Boxers you are presented, remembering that many of the cosmetic issues, such as poor coat or thinness, will remedy themselves as the Boxer begins its life of good food, exercise, and care. Also, keep an open line of communication between you and the rescue. This is the dog you will be caring for during the next eight or more years. It should be the one you want and the one that brings that zany Boxer joy into your life. Make sure the match is right.

Contracts and papers: Once you've found your bouncing canine pretzel, you're not through yet. There is a bit of paperwork you should receive and a contract that must be signed before you can take your Boxer home.

You should receive a copy of the dog's veterinary work, detailing vaccinations and wormings, verification of spay/neuter, and results of any tests, such as a blood test for heartworm. You may also receive a copy of the dog's information sheet from its previous owner, detailing the reasons for the dog's surrender. You may not be able to see the transfer of ownership paper, but you should have the presence of this document

verified. The transfer of ownership prevents the dog's former owner from trying to reclaim the dog at a later date.

As for contracts, the one you will sign may have several stipulations in it. The first is that if you are unable to keep the Boxer, or if your care is not satisfactory, Boxer Rescue retains the right to take back the dog. There may also be a clause in the contract that requires you to keep your dog on a leash while outside or in a safe, fenced yard. Again, violation of this stipulation could cost you the dog.

The contract will contain a clause that limits the liability of the rescue. This clause says that you, the adopter, agree to hold the rescue harmless of any damages the adopted dog causes. If your adopted Boxer shreds your favorite couch one afternoon, you cannot hold Boxer Rescue liable for the replacement of the couch. Basically, this clause is the "it's-your-dog-now" clause that places the responsibility on you for the dog's actions.

Follow-up visits: Once you have your adopted Boxer, you won't be left hanging. Boxer Rescue is similar to a big family. Rescue volunteers will check on you from time to time to make sure your Boxer is adjusting well to its new life. If you have any questions regarding care or training, these people are the folks to ask. Their sincerest hopes are that you and your Boxer are partners for the life of the dog. They will go to all ends, it seems, to make sure they are there for you.

Additionally, you'll find the rescue family is a bit of a social group. Many local rescues hold annual picnics and other activities where everyone brings their dogs, eats, plays games, and has a really fun time. Some rescues print newsletters that are sent to all adopters to keep them informed of the rescue's goings-on and upcoming events. It's a great group to be associated with, and it's also great fun for your dog.

Keeping tabs: If you adopt a Boxer from rescue, don't forget to send your local group a photo of your happy Boxer in its new home. Nothing makes a rescue happier than knowing their Boxers are doing well. Many rescues keep scrapbooks of their rescues—and most remember each dog *by name*.

Breeders

Though few people consider consulting with a breeder for dogs other than puppies, a quality breeder may also be a source for an adult Boxer. Occasionally, a breeder may have an adult Boxer that had been reserved for the show ring or a performance event and the dog just didn't turn out according to the breeder's expectations. The dog is older and not a puppy, so it is not as easy to find a home for it. Mind you, this dog is probably a knockout as far as looks, because it is considered an "almost" show dog.

Since this dog grew up with a quality breeder, it has been properly socialized, habituated to everyday living and certainly car travel, and

trained beyond just being a "good" dog. This Boxer will be calm and still for baths, toenail trimming, ear cleaning, and veterinary exams. It will also walk on a leash with little pull—in the show ring dogs are not allowed to pull their handlers around—stand rock solid when given a *stand* or *stay* command, and will allow total strangers to check its teeth, legs, and body, just as a judge would do in the show ring.

The breeder's adult dog will also have been fed a quality diet, and, depending on its age, it may have been screened and certified "negative" or free (hopefully) for several diseases. The breeder's adult Boxer will not come without a price, of course, but you can see the many advantages to obtaining an adult dog from a source such as this.

The breeder may also have another type of adult dog available. If the breeder stands behind his or her breeding, the breeder will take back any Boxer that he or she has bred for any reason and at any age. This includes Boxers that are suddenly without a home because of the owner's death or perhaps a divorce. Dogs are sometimes returned because their dander is discovered to be causing serious allergies in the owner's new baby. Since quality breeders really try to screen their prospective puppy owners very closely, most dogs are returned for good reasons. These dogs are generally fine family pets that have had some training and most likely are house-trained. The breeder knows the dogs' history and temperament well, so there isn't much guesswork involved in evaluating them.

Again, a quality breeder's adult dogs can make great pets—perhaps even potential show dogs. There have been recorded cases when a returned dog had developed into something exceptional and the new owner finished a championship and campaigned the dog as a special quite successfully.

A word of warning: Not all breeders are quality breeders (see Chapter Four). Purchasing an adult dog from a less-than-reputable breeder could mean a whole pack of trouble. Puppy farmers sell off old brood bitches when the poor things can't produce puppies anymore. These dogs have been caged and socially isolated most of their lives. This dog can be exceptionally difficult to turn around. It is best not to purchase such a dog.

Shelters and Pounds

This is the time-honored way of adopting an adult dog—through your local city pound or area humane organization. Depending on the services provided by your area shelters and pounds, your experiences trying to adopt a Boxer from these facilities can be either marvelous or less than memorable.

The ideal shelter or pound offers a comprehensive evaluation of the dog's health and temperament when it enters the shelter and doesn't rely on the surrendering owner's questionnaire answers. One would

A rescued Boxer is just waiting to find the right owner with whom to share its unending love.

assume that the dog's owner would want to make his or her dog look like the ideal canine citizen in order to increase the dog's chances of being adopted. Shelter officials say, however, that the opposite is true; owners frequently write down that their dogs are impossible to house-train or have aggression problems *just to give themselves a "good" reason for turning in the dog.* If you are looking at a Boxer in an adoption facility that doesn't evaluate the dog's temperament, be sure to take a trainer or an experienced Boxer breeder with you to properly evaluate the dog.

As for the dog's health, there are shelters and pounds that offer extensive veterinary services, including spaying or neutering before the dog leaves the facility. The dogs are also wormed, vaccinated (if the dog has no vaccination record), and tested for heartworm prior to the adoption. Contrast this to shelter facilities that do not have the funds to perform these services and simply release the dog "as is" for a sum of money.

Some nonprofit shelters even offer dog ownership counseling services, require some screening of potential owners, and provide training classes for new dog owners. Municipal pounds generally can't afford these luxuries and focus their attention on treating the dogs humanely until they are either adopted or euthanized.

The key to remember when adopting a dog from a shelter or pound is that before you bring the new dog into your home have a pro-fessional trainer, experienced breeder, or veterinarian evaluate the Boxer's temperament. If the dog looks like it will be a good pet, then, before you take it home, schedule a complete veterinary checkup, a spay/neuter (an overnighter), followed by a visit to the groomer. This way, you can bring home a clean, vaccinated, and altered Boxer that is ready to begin its new life.

Don't forget the crate! Yes, you already love your newly adopted Boxer, but it must earn your trust. On the way home from the shelter or pound, be sure to crate your Boxer. There have been stories of usually peaceful dogs going berserk in the car and nearly causing an accident. Also, you don't know if the dog will get carsick or not, or if it is perhaps suffering from intestinal distress. Avoid problems, and crate the Boxer in the car.

If you visit a shelter or pound several times but don't see any Boxers, there may be a reason why. Many of these facilities work in concert with local Boxer Rescues. In these shelters and pounds, when a Boxer is surrendered, the facility immediately calls an official with the Boxer Rescue in that area. The shelter or pound knows the dog will be well cared for and placed in a good, permanent home and the shelter will have the room to take in another dog. This cooperative relationship benefits Boxer Rescue, too, in that rescue volunteers don't have to check the shelters and pounds on a frequent basis for Boxers and can

Don't worry too much about missing the puppy antics of your adult Boxer; your rescue Boxer will provide you with many playful moments for years to come.

spend their time in more productive areas, such as placement activities.

A Word on Kids and Dogs

Unless a Boxer has been severely mistreated or unsocialized with children, these dogs generally make wonderful family pets. Their temperament is downright silly at times, and the more a child wants to play, the more the Boxer will play. The greatest danger with Boxers and children is the potential for this exuberant, muscular dog to accidentally bowl over a smaller child. They tend to be very forgiving and seem to have a high threshold of pain (in case a child falls on them).

Dog Bites

• How common are dog bites? An estimated 31.2 million families own dogs in the United States. Each year, more than 4.7 million Americans are bitten by a dog, with an estimated 800,000 of these incidents requiring emergency room treatment.
• Who gets bitten? Children. The vast majority of those bitten are children under the age of 12.
• Who's doing the biting? Not strays. Not feral dogs. Studies indicate that the dogs doing the biting are *owned* by someone. Many of the bites are sustained by family members from the family pet.

No dog, especially if not well known by the owner, *should ever be left alone with children.* If you cannot closely supervise your Boxer with your children, then you must be able to separate them. If you cannot separate them, then you should not have a Boxer. With any adopted dog, you must never assume anything. You must make the dog *prove* it can be trusted.

With a rescued Boxer, you're guaranteed to have a ball.

Unconditional love.

Remember, you didn't raise this dog from puppyhood. You don't know its life experiences. You do not know everything about this dog's past. Most important, you do not know its threshold for biting. The power and shape of the Boxer's jaws make a bite from this breed a near-guaranteed trip to the emergency room. So, even if you've adopted the sweetest Boxer in the world, don't take anything for granted around your children.

Teach your children the following rules around the Boxer:

1. Don't pet a dog while it is sleeping. Wake it first by calling its name.

2. Respect the dog's crate. This is its special area and is not for children.

3. Do not pet the dog while it is eating or try to take a bone away from it.

4. Don't roughhouse with the dog.

5. Be kind to your Boxer and it will be your closest companion.

Chapter Six

Preparing for the New Arrival

Whether you are adopting an adult Boxer or purchasing a puppy, you will need to prepare your home and family as best you can. Since Boxers really never grow up—they just get a little gray—both future adult and puppy owners need to make sure their homes and yards are safe for the new arrival. Because the Boxer is quick and agile, and don't forget clever, this job can be a little more involved than perhaps with a more complacent breed.

Preparing your home and taking a proactive stance in Boxer care can be the single best way to avoid much of the stress of introducing a new dog or puppy into the home. It will cut down on the possibility for much of the destruction associated with an active puppy or inquisitive adult, and the structure will help the dog or puppy to settle into its new life even quicker.

What to Do in Advance

There are two things you must do well in advance of picking up your new Boxer: schedule an appointment with your veterinarian, and register for training classes.

Veterinarian

If you are purchasing a puppy, make sure to schedule the veterinary appointment on your way home from the breeder's, if possible. If this isn't possible, make sure this appointment is made within three days tops, even if the breeder says the puppy isn't due for any vaccinations and has just been wormed. The reason this first appointment is so important is that you want your trusted veterinarian to give you a very honest evaluation of the condition—both physical and mental—of your puppy. You also want your veterinarian to give the puppy a complete and thorough health exam before you take it home. Thus, if your veterinarian detects any serious health or temperament problems with the puppy, you will know this immediately and may decide to return the puppy before you've passed the point of no return with your heart. Also, if you have other animals or dogs at home, it is important to make sure the

Before your Boxer will be a truly wonderful housedog, you must commit to fully training it.

puppy is not harboring any communicable diseases.

This first visit to the veterinarian is very important with an adult Boxer, too, especially if the dog has been adopted from a shelter or pound with very few services available to adopters. Even if you have received your dog from Boxer Rescue, the veterinarian should be your first stop on the way home. As mentioned previously, if you've adopted an adult from a shelter or pound, your

second stop, after seeing the veterinarian, should be the groomer so that your Boxer is free of ticks and fleas and smells good.

Along with a physical exam, if you are adopting an adult Boxer, this is the time to get your dog spayed or neutered. Unless your Boxer is particularly weak and needs some rehabilitation, or your veterinarian suggests delaying the procedure for another reason, get it done now! You will be able to pick up your Boxer the very next day and begin a wonderful life together.

Training Classes

One thing that many new puppy and adult dog owners forget in the excitement of bringing a new Boxer home is the importance of registering for a training class *before the dog comes home.* Puppy preschool or kindergarten classes fill up very quickly and are generally offered in cycles of six or eight weeks. If you miss the chance to sign up, you'll have to wait until the next training cycle. This could be the difference between training a small 12-week-old puppy and working with a strapping 5-month-old Boxer.

If you're adopting an adult Boxer, it is equally important to enroll in a basic or beginner's obedience class. Even if your Boxer is well trained, it is important to begin training class to develop a close relationship with the dog and to confirm—or reconfirm—who is the leader and who is the Boxer. If your Boxer has had little training or has some behavioral challenges, beginning a training class and working with a professional trainer becomes even more important.

Whether you are purchasing a puppy or adopting an adult dog, you'll find that a solid course of training will help deepen the bond between you and your Boxer, as well as provide you with a support group for all sorts of training and non-training questions (see the chapter on training the Boxer, Chapter Twelve, for more information on finding a good training center).

Supplies You Will Need

You've set up your appointment with the veterinarian and have a space reserved in the next training class; now it's time to make sure you have all the supplies you'll need for your new Boxer. If you're lucky, you live in a town with a pet store that never closes, so if you forget something or discover you're running low on a critical dog product, you can run out to the store and get what you need. However, it's really a good idea to plan ahead so that for the first few days you can enjoy your new pet and not worry about running back and forth to the store for supplies.

The following is a basic list of supplies most commonly needed in those first few days and weeks of new Boxer ownership.

Collar

Your Boxer will need a collar when you bring it home from the breeder or rescue. Do not buy a choke chain or any other collar that functions as a choke chain for your puppy or adult's "everyday" collar; in most instances, you will not need this type of collar even when you are training your Boxer. A collar like this is guaranteed to catch on something and strangle your dog. Boxers have been known to strangle themselves on their collars in the "safety" of their own crates.

If you are purchasing a puppy, an efficient collar is one that expands over several sizes. Your puppy will grow by leaps and bounds in its first year and will go through several collar sizes before it is fully grown. With an expandable collar, you can keep adjusting it as your puppy grows. You'll want to be careful, however, to make sure that the collar is properly adjusted and fastened so that the excess collar is firmly held in place and does not create a choking hazard.

Flat-buckle collars are good choices for both puppies and adults and can be purchased in nylon, a tough cotton web, and leather. Though leather collars are generally the gentlest on the dog's coat, they are a bit more expensive and seem to be considered a particularly attractive snack or chew item among both puppies and adults. If your Boxer chews through a cotton web collar, you may be less upset than if it devours a pricier collar, so if you are purchasing a collar, it may be more frugal to purchase collars of less expensive materials while your puppy is growing and save the expensive collar for when it is fully grown.

Leash

Your Boxer should always be walked on a leash. Even very young puppies should be kept on a leash when they aren't in a protected, fenced backyard. Though they look small and appear to want to stay very close to you, there is no way you can catch one of these little guys when they decide to take off. If they dash about and fall into the path of an oncoming car, you will never forgive yourself for your negligence. *Buy a leash.*

Older children can learn about dog ownership and become involved in the dog's training and care.

With that said, there are several options when it comes to leashes. The simplest is the standard 6-foot (1.8-m) leash with a snap attachment that hooks to the dog's collar. Leashes come in nylon, heavy cotton web, and leather. Nylon is tough, but if your dog is a bit unruly before it is fully trained, this material can really tear up your hands. Cotton web won't give you the burns of a nylon leash. Leather is a good material, but remember that it is slick and hard to hold when it is wet, so if you are walking your dog in the rain and don't have your hand looped through the grip, you may be chasing after your Boxer dragging its leash.

Beyond the standard leash, another popular favorite is the retractable leash. This leash extends and retracts as the dog pulls. It can also be "locked" at a certain length. Until you have your Boxer trained to walk nicely on a leash, this probably is not the best leash to have. If your Boxer is zinging in and out at will, you won't be able to teach it to stay by your side. Even in the locked position, this hard plastic container and handle for this leash is a bit bulky to hold. The leash is wonderful, however, if you want to allow your Boxer a little freedom. For example, if you are going to the beach for a walk and you want to let your dog splash in the waves without having to go in yourself or allowing it off leash, a 30-foot (9-m) retractable leash is perfect. If you purchase this leash for your dog, be sure to buy the grade for heavy or very strong dogs. If you buy a cheaper, lighter-weight version, your Boxer may very well hit the end, break the leash and keep going.

Note: Avoid leashes made of metal links with a leather loop handle. In addition to being impractical to hold correctly for obedience training, they also portray the wrong image for both you and your dog.

Crate

This is something you just can't do without. You will need a crate for traveling in the car, and you will need a crate to safely confine your puppy or new adult when you can't be at home to supervise it. Crates are also very helpful in teaching house-training manners (see page 00), so the question is not whether to purchase a crate or not, but which crate to purchase and in what size.

Size: If you're adopting an adult Boxer, you'll have no problem deciding what size crate to get; since you know the exact size of your Boxer, you don't have to guess the size of the crate. The crate should be big enough for the dog to stand up, turn around, and lie down comfortably.

If you are purchasing a puppy, you can only guess what you will eventually need. What the puppy fits today, it will not fit in the next month or two. A crate that fits the puppy and is not too big often helps to expedite the house-training process. Boxers prefer to be dry and clean

A crate is essential in acclimating your puppy or adult to its new home.

and will prefer to "hold it" than to be near a mess. When using a crate of this size—not overly big—the owner must be very vigilant in heeding the puppy's need for frequent and regular relief. If using an adult crate, many styles offer partitions that can be fastened in order to make the crate just the right size. Regardless of your set-up, the puppy should not be in the crate for more than 8 to 10 hours during a 24-hour period.

To figure out what size crate your puppy might eventually grow into, ask your breeder his or her opinion. If your puppy is a larger male, it may eventually need a large crate. If you are selecting the runt of the litter, it may never outgrow a medium crate; then again, it may grow a lot while in

Crates can be lined with a pad or soft blanket for your adult Boxer that knows how to behave.

folded up into a compact space when not in use, and its airiness makes it cooler on warm days. One of the disadvantages of this type of crate is that because it is so open, some dogs and puppies do not feel comfortable or protected. Also, they tend to be a bit more expensive, particularly if they are collapsible and have a coating that is not dangerous to dogs and prevents rusting. This type of crate is not approved for shipping on an airline, either.

The hard-shell plastic crates, however, are approved for shipping via air cargo, so if this is ever a remote possibility, you've got this angle covered without having to purchase another crate. The solid plastic crates also give a dog a more protected, denlike feeling because they have no wire mesh except for the door to the crate and a few side ventilation panels. These crates can be lined with paper for puppies, or a fitted pad or soft blanket for the adult that behaves well in a crate. The disadvantage to the plastic crates is that they are not as airy as the wire crates and therefore do not provide as much air circulation. They are a bit warmer in the winter than a wire crate, and are quite a bit warmer in the summer. As long as your crate is in a cool spot in your home, this shouldn't be a problem. Another consideration with this type of crate is that it doesn't collapse for storage, if you no longer need it on a regular basis.

Unfortunately, manufacturers don't make either style crate in

your care and require a larger crate. Don't fuss too much over this issue. The worst situation is that if you err on the small side, you will just have to buy another crate.

Type: The type of crate you purchase can be important in helping your new Boxer settle into its new life. Crates generally come in two styles: wire and plastic. The wire crates are very open and have a metal pan at the bottom that can be layered with sheets of newsprint and a thick layer of shredded newspaper for a puppy, or a soft pad for an adult that doesn't chew, shred, or fluff when it is bored. The advantages to this crate are that it can be

designer colors or natural woods that might blend in with the rest of your home's decor. These crates, much like your Boxer, will shout "Here I am!" in almost any room you put them in.

Baby Gates

If you plan to limit your Boxer's activities to one easily cleaned room that contains little of anything of value that can be destroyed, you will need a way to safely contain your puppy or adult in this area. Baby gates come in a variety of styles and heights and can either be permanently attached to your wall—be sure to find the studs and not just the drywall—or temporarily attached using pressure to lock them into place. There are some gates made specifically for dogs and are nearly double the height of a regular gate. They are made to expand to a variety of different widths, but be sure to measure the area you want gated to make sure the style you choose will work in that area.

Identification

Dog owners often forget that one of the most likely times for a dog to get lost is when it first comes home. Puppies have no idea where they are or how to find their way back home, and adults in a new area will be equally confused if they get lost. Before you go to pick up your new Boxer, make sure to have a tag made that is engraved with the following: "I am a Boxer," followed by your address and phone number with area code. The area code is important because adult dogs can travel miles out of the area in a relatively short time. Once you've brought your puppy or adult home and have decided on a name, you can have a new tag engraved with the Boxer's name and other information. You may also consider putting "Reward" on the tag to encourage finders to call. Then you need to consider a permanent means of identification, either through tattooing or microchipping.

Tattoos: When people tattoo their dogs, they aren't talking about getting a picture of a poodle etched onto the chest of their dogs. And you don't have to go to a tattoo parlor to get the service done. Tattoing pets as a means of permanent identification is growing in the United States. Tattoo registries report phenomenal rates of recovery when a pet is identified by a tattoo. The procedure is relatively painless; the dog doesn't even have to be anesthetized. Tattoos can, however, fade with age or get "stretched" as a puppy grows, to the point that it's illegible. Tattoos are best for near-adult or adult dogs. The number should be registered with a national registry and the dog should wear a tag that says "I have a tattoo" with the phone number of the registry engraved on the tag.

Microchips: Microchips are about the size of a grain of rice and are implanted between the dog's shoulder blades. This is a veterinary procedure and, according to implanters,

These Boxers need tags for proper identification in case they escape the yard and get lost.

is only momentarily uncomfortable when the chip is injected under the skin. Each chip has its own code and when the dog is scanned with a chip reader, the number will pop up. Shelters across the country have scanners and many use them regularly. The problem with chips right now is that the average person who might find your dog would never know that your dog was chipped, or perhaps even what microchip identification is. If you live in an area in which chipping clinics are provided by the area shelters and your shelters do, in fact, scan for these chips, this might be a good option for your dog. But be aware that in some instances the chip can travel under your dog's skin to a place where a scanner won't pick up the presence of the chip.

For further information on tattooing and microchipping, your best source of information is your veterinarian who can discuss additional pros and cons of each form of identification and help you to make the best decision for your Boxer.

Newspapers, Old Towels

Start collecting newspapers now. Forget the recycle bin; your very own personal little recycler is on its way. You'll need plenty of fresh papers to line the Boxer's crate for quite a while.

Go through your linen closet and pull out any towels that are wearing out. Your Boxer won't mind if they have a few holes in them or aren't super plush, as long as they're cuddly. Towels are easier to wash than expensive pads or crate liners, and they can be pawed and tugged at until they have been molded into a suitable little bed. If you find your Boxer is a shredder, however, you may just want to stick to newspaper and leave your stash of towels for baths.

Food and Bowls

Your Boxer needs to eat. Be sure to ask the breeder or rescue what type of food your Boxer is accustomed to and purchase a sizeable bag of this food. If you plan to change the dog over to a different food, wait a week or so and then begin mixing parts of the new food in until the transition has been made (see Nutrition, page 126). Of course, you'll need bowls for both your dog's food and its water. Heavy non-tipping bowls are best and tend to minimize cleanups after meals. (They also discourage your Boxer from galloping around the backyard with a food bowl in its jaws and then using it as a major chew bone.

Treats

Gotta have some treats. You'll need these primarily for training. Prepackaged treats for dogs are good, but owners can also chop up bits of dried liver or even carrots. Treats should be healthful, and chopped into small pieces so that you can reward your dog often throughout the day without stuffing it.

Toys, Toys, and More Toys

Your puppy or adult Boxer will need a lot of toys; Boxers live by the credo: "I may have to grow older but no one said I had to act maturely!" You will need to be careful in purchasing appropriate toys for your puppy or adult. Because the Boxer has a very powerful jaw and "bite," and because it *loves* to chew and rip and tear at its toys, the toy must be virtually indestructible. It must also be big enough that it can't be swallowed or have pieces that might break off that could be swallowed. There have been entire articles written on what types of items have been removed from the stomachs of dogs. And finally, the toys must be large enough that the puppy or adult cannot try to swallow it and choke on it instead.

Tug-of-war: Your Boxer will love to play tug-of-war with you. There are a variety of tug toys on the market that make this game even more fun; however, playing tug-of-war with a strong and toothy dog such as the Boxer has come under some criticism. Critics of tug games say this teaches the dog to be dominant-aggressive with humans and encourages "biting and holding." Proponents of tug games say this is nonsense and it depends on the dog.

What to do? If your dog shows any signs of aggression—dominance or territorial—this game should not be encouraged. In a dog that shows no aggression whatsoever, even when playing with children, the right choice is probably less well defined. To decide what is best for your Boxer and your family, consult with your veterinarian and your trainer, both professionals who know your dog's temperament and your dog-handling experience. They can help you make sure you're not accidentally teaching your Boxer the wrong behaviors.

Anti-chew Salve and Sprays

These concoctions are made by several manufacturers and come in a variety of nasty flavors. The purpose is to use this substance on things you don't want your Boxer to chew on in your home. For the most part, it's effective, except with Boxers that lack taste. Check your pet-supply store.

Stain Remover/Enzyme Eater

There will inevitably be a few accidents so it's good to have a supply of pet stain and odor remover on hand to immediately attack any indiscretions your Boxer may make on your carpeting or furniture. Again, look in your pet-supply store.

Grooming Brushes, Nail Clippers

While you are warming up that credit card with all the other pet store purchases, you might as well invest in a nice set of grooming supplies. A good natural bristle brush and toenail clippers should do it for now.

Purchases for You

Now that you've invested a small fortune in supplies for the new Boxer, what else is there to buy?

Film for the camera is one purchase you shouldn't forget. Puppies grow quickly and rescued adults rehab rapidly. Be sure to have a roll of film, or two or three, and a ready camera to capture those photo moments.

Also, read up on as many books on puppy care and training as you can get your hands on. Books focusing on puppy problems are useful in that they give you a heads up as to potential problems in your home. A few favorite books are listed in Useful Addresses and Literature (see page 196).

Boxer-proofing Your Home

To keep down the level of turmoil a new Boxer can bring as it charges into your life, you'll want to take some precautions in your home. The purpose for this is twofold: You'll want to limit the potential destruction a puppy or adult can inflict on your home furnishings, and you'll want to safeguard your Boxer from hurting itself.

Electrical cords: Get these out of sight and out of reach. If your Boxer

A Boxer's life is never long enough; make sure you Boxer-proof your home and yard to avoid a deadly accident.

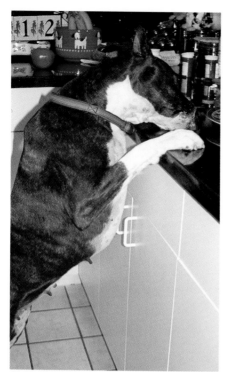

Counters are fair game and dinner is irresistible. Keep foods out of reach of your Boxer.

If you want to keep your Boxer out of the garbage, move it behind closed doors.

gets its teeth on an electrical cord, it will either pull over a lamp or chew through the cord and can kill itself. If it partially chews through the cord, you now have an electrical fire hazard. For cords that can't be hidden, try a plastic runner designed specifically for cords on flooring or, if the cord is in a visible spot, you could apply a no-chew product that is foul tasting but harmless.

Shoes: Puppies and adults don't know the difference between their toys and yours. Therefore, your shoes, clothes, briefcase, television

remote, and other items that you may be used to leaving around the house are fair game for chewing. Anything you don't want your Boxer to turn into a canine toy should be kept out of reach of your Boxer.

Counter patrol: Jumping on the kitchen counter is a snap for a full-grown Boxer, or even an adolescent. Boxers have a tremendous sense of smell—they can be very good at tracking and are used as drug-sniffing dogs—so don't think your dog won't notice that box of fresh donuts on the counter. Nor should you ever believe the innocent, pious look your Boxer gives you as it rests peacefully on its bed. As soon as you leave the room, the donuts will be his!

Garbage lockout: So many people complain, "My Boxer is driving me crazy! He's always knocking over the garbage can and strewing garbage everywhere. What can I do to get him to stop this?" This one has an easy solution: Put the garbage away. Do not leave it out for your Boxer to eat. It's not good for the dog, and it's probably not good for your blood pressure. If your Boxer learns to open the cabinet doors to the garbage can, bungee cord them shut if you have to or move the receptacle to a room with a door and firmly shut the door.

Table decorations/breakables: The Boxer is a joyful, exuberant dog. Love your Boxer for this and, to avoid the heartbreak of some cherished memento crashing into a zillion little pieces, move your breakables to higher ground. Maybe this is the time to splurge on that curio cabinet you've always wanted.

Upholstered furnishings: Before your Boxer joins your family, decide in advance if it will be allowed on the couches (because it will surely ask), and if so, which couches are allowable and which aren't. To avoid having a hairy couch, put a pet throw or an easily washed blanket on the couch. Also, remember that not all Boxers can be trusted to sleep peacefully on a sofa when no one is watching. Left unattended, a Boxer can wreak havoc in a very short time.

Carpets: Until your Boxer is completely house-trained, it is a good idea to limit its carpet time to only that period just after it has relieved itself, and while it is being closely supervised.

Deadly Everyday Products

Many everyday consumer products are poisonous if consumed in even small quantities by your puppy or adult dog. These products have child-safe packaging; however, child-safe is not Boxer-proof! Here are some products that should be kept away from your Boxer.

Toilet cleaners/fresheners: Blue water is not healthy for your dog to drink. And, since it's a given that a Boxer will drink from the toilet if the seat is up—even if there's a fresh, cool bowl of water set out—make sure there's nothing in the toilet water that could jeopardize the health of your dog. Toilet bowl cleaners that release chemicals with every flush are not a good idea around dogs. If you feel you must use these products, keep the lid down at all times and the door to the lavatory firmly shut.

Roach motels/pesticides/rodenticides: These products contain some serious chemicals that should always be kept away from your puppy or dog. It won't take much of these products to kill a Boxer. The products also seem to be attractive in taste and smell to dogs, so don't count on your Boxer leaving the little roach motel alone behind the couch. If creepy crawlies or mice are a problem in your home or yard, you will need to consult with your veterinarian and a professional exterminator for advice on how to handle the situation.

Cleaning liquids: Don't assume that because you keep your floor, counter, and bathroom cleaning fluids under the sink and behind closed doors that these products are squirreled safely from your Boxer. If your Boxer figures out how to open your cabinets, or if you leave these products out, your Boxer could be in very serious trouble. Make sure the cabinets containing these cleaners are either up high where the Boxer can't get to them, or behind doors that can't be opened by the dog.

Medicines: Prescription and over-the-counter medications should be kept out of reach of your puppy or adult Boxer at all times. This includes such innocuous products as medicated shampoos, toothpaste, and sunscreens. None of these products were designed to be eaten.

Antifreeze: It only takes a very small amount to leak or spill from your car and your Boxer will die if it laps the fluid up. This product is very poisonous and has been the cause of many dogs' painful deaths. Be careful!

Boxer-proofing Your Yard

Your home is not the only area you will need to prepare for the new arrival; you will also need to Boxer-proof your yard. The most critical aspect here is to have a safe fence. Not only do you need to have a

A sturdy, tall fence is a must for keeping your Boxer safe at home.

If you own a swimming pool, make sure your Boxers know how to use the steps to exit the pool and only allow swimming while you are watching.

fence to keep your dog in, but also to keep other dogs and people out.

Liability on a Chain

A dog chained to a stake in an open yard is not an acceptable means of keeping a dog. A chained dog is not only at risk of choking but it is isolated socially, too. When socially deprived, even a normally well-behaved Boxer can develop into a frantic and perhaps aggressive animal. A dog such as this is no pleasure to own and is, in fact, a liability. If another dog or a child crosses your property within range of the staked dog's chain, and the dog has developed a bad attitude (territorial, dominance, and/or dog aggression), the safety of those crossing your property could very well be in jeopardy.

If the city or state has a dangerous dog law, the owner of a dog that bites is held accountable for that dog's actions. Depending on the city or state laws, owning a dangerous or vicious dog can result in heavy fines and jail time.

Fences

What type of fence is best for your Boxer? A tall, sturdy one would be one good answer. Both wooden privacy fences and heavy chain-link can work well in a backyard. Which style you choose depends on your tastes, the size of your pocketbook, and what the fencing restrictions are in your neighborhood. Boxers are athletic, and if determined, can scale seemingly impossible fences. They can also dig under a well-built fence, so make sure that the fence extends flush with the ground to hopefully discourage any escape artist efforts by your dog.

Hidden electrical fences that work in concert with a collar are effective to a point. While your power is on, the fence is operational. If your power goes out, during an electrical storm, for instance, your fence is now "down." Your Boxer is probably gone, too. Another disadvantage to consider with this type of fence is that it allows other animals and people to come into your yard. Depending on the temperament of your Boxer, this may not be a good thing.

If you have an existing wood or chain-link fence, be sure to walk the entire length of it looking for loose or protruding nails, missing boards, or torn wire. Be sure to make these repairs now before your Boxer finds them and accidentally injures itself. Also, invest in a padlock for your gate. Someone who knows how friendly your Boxer is may be tempted to steal it. A padlock may not prevent a theft, but it will help to discourage it. It also will help to discourage children from opening and perhaps not shutting your gate, letting your beloved Boxer loose.

Poisonous Plants

Many common annuals, perennials, bulbs, shrubs, and even trees are poisonous to dogs if eaten. Some plant poisons cause a minor irritation; others can kill your Boxer with just a small taste. Your veterinarian should have a complete list of toxic plants that you can keep as a reference. If your dog or puppy eats a plant and you're not sure what the plant was or if it is toxic, take whatever part of the plant you find, along with the dog, to the veterinarian's office as soon as possible. It's better to be safe than to have a severely ill or dead dog.

Pools

Do you have a pool in the backyard? Some Boxers enjoy a dip; others don't. If your Boxer enjoys swimming and you are going to allow it in your pool, make sure it knows where the steps are to get out of the pool. Dogs have drowned after jumping into a pool for a swim and then not knowing how to get out.

If your Boxer doesn't enjoy swimming, and you can't show it how to safely exit the pool, make sure it can't get near the pool. Keep it outside the pool's fenced area as you would any unsupervised child. Accidents do happen, and generally when you're not looking. One slip while running around the pool could drown a Boxer or a young pup.

Prepare Your Family

If you live alone, the only person you need to prepare for the new Boxer is yourself. If you are married, however, live with a roommate, have

Boxers are always ready for fun.

children or older parents in the same home, you will need to have a "family talk" to clearly outline which family members will be charged with which chores. In addition, you'll want to make sure everyone understands which rooms the puppy or adult Boxer is allowed in and which rooms are forbidden—and decide now whether the Boxer is allowed on couches and chairs or not. And, learn what types of snacks are allowed and what types will upset your Boxer's stomach. Rules on shutting doors and gates may need to be revisited with younger children, and you should have a serious discussion about how to treat a dog kindly. In a home with multiple owners, cooperation and consistency are the keys.

Kids and Chores

What is the right age to give a child the responsibility of caring for and owning a Boxer? The answer is: It depends on the child. If a child must be reminded to brush her teeth at night or to take a bath, this child cannot be expected to remember to feed the dog without supervision. With children under the age of 13 or so, direct parental involvement is necessary for the welfare of the Boxer.

Older teenagers may very well be responsible enough to care for a puppy or an adult Boxer, but parents will find that they still need to "be there" for the Boxer. Teenagers have pretty active lives with after-school practices, club meetings, and social lives. Your teen may very well be capable of caring for a dog, but may not be at home to perform all the chores, all the time.

Young children should never be expected to care for a dog by themselves; however, teaming with a parent can make a great learning experience and give you, the parent, precious "together" time with your child.

The bottom line with children and their responsibility is that to have a successful pet in the home, the parent must take an active role in the dog's care. This may mean keeping an eye out when your teen feeds the Boxer, or it may mean actively reminding your ten-year-old to freshen the dog's water every day. If a parent is not willing to be the underlying force in the raising of the Boxer, then now is not the right time to have a dog. Wait until you have the time and desire to participate.

Schedule Time Off

Your home, yard, and family are ready for the new arrival—but are you? Make sure you are well rested before the Boxer arrives, because you may not get much sleep for the next few days. If you can, schedule the pickup of your puppy or dog so that you can visit the veterinarian and have it back home for the weekend. Better yet, if possible, why not take a week off from work so that you can be with the Boxer and help it adjust to its new lifestyle? That way, if you're up at night because your puppy is a bit upset about leaving its littermates or, in the case of an adult, everything is just so new, you'll need the days off to catch up on your sleep.

Ready, Set, Go Get That Boxer

Once you bring that puppy or adult Boxer home, there's no looking back. You're ready, you're educated, and you know what your commitment level must be to make this relationship work. You've made all the necessary preparations to set your Boxer up for success in its new life. Without a doubt, you're ready to pick up your Boxer and begin a memorable and treasured canine-human partnership.

Chapter Seven

The Boxer's Life Stages

While it takes humans 20 years to reach physical maturity, a Boxer puppy will mature in just 18 months. The road to maturity is filled with adventure. As your puppy matures, it will go through several milestones in its physical and emotional development. The path is not always smooth; there will be a few bumps in the road, if only to keep the Boxer owner on his or her toes. With a good understanding of how your puppy develops and an awareness of the critical stages through which the puppy will pass, the Boxer owner increases his or her-ability to raise a socially responsible adult Boxer that is a sheer joy to live with.

Prenatal

The puppy begins its life as a tiny speck developing in its mother's uterus. It will take roughly two months for the embryo to develop into a fetus that is ready to be born. During this development period, it is critical that the Boxer mother is well cared for both physically and emo-

tionally. Prior to breeding, the bitch should have been screened by a veterinarian for a variety of diseases and conditions that could affect her ability to conceive and possibly affect the health of her puppies. In addition, the prospective mother Boxer should be up to date on her shots and recently wormed. While the puppies are developing, her nutritional requirements increase, and experienced breeders are careful to make sure the pregnant dog's needs are met.

A healthy Boxer is not enough, say researchers, in developing healthy puppies. The treatment of the pregnant mother and her emotional state during her pregnancy has a strong influence on the future social abilities of the puppies. Imprinting, it appears, begins *before the puppies are even born.* In one study, it was shown that petting and stroking the mother had a significant effect on the puppies' future tolerance to being touched. A conscientious breeder, therefore, can facilitate the *good* attributes in his or her puppies. This is one more reason that it is critical to

Puppies are born with their eyes closed, minimal hearing, and a natural instinct to suckle.

be very selective in choosing a breeder from which to purchase your Boxer puppy. Likewise, keeping his breeding stock isolated in a cage under marginal conditions in a "puppy farm," with minimal human contact, can have detrimental effects on the ensuing puppies. A poorly kept, stressful mother will transmit, to some degree, her poor physical and emotional health to her puppies.

Neonatal

When the puppies are born, they are totally dependent on their mother. Weighing less than a pound, their eyes are not open, and, though this theory may be reversed with future research, newly whelped puppies are thought to have limited capabilities of learning. They react to the scent of their mother's milk, know innately how to suckle, and can cry, whimper, and growl. Being physically near their mother is important in keeping the puppies warm.

Newborn puppies have limited mobility in these very early days and move by dragging themselves around. An exceptionally large litter—more than seven puppies—may require the assistance of the breeder through supplemental bottle-feeding of some puppies to make sure all of them are getting enough to eat. Bottle-feeding puppies is an arduous chore but must be undertaken if a mother is having problems with her milk supply or if she develops a mammary infection.

Puppies that are eating well and are healthy can be expected to double their birth weight within eight to nine days. The puppies' "milk" teeth also appear during these first few days.

In countries where docking is legal, the puppies' tails are severed by a veterinarian around the third or fourth day of life. At this time, if the puppies' dewclaws—the fifth toe located on the inside of each front leg—are to be removed, the veterinarian performs this procedure, too.

The Young Puppy: Two to Sixteen Weeks

By the time the Boxer puppy is two weeks old, its eyes are open and within a few days it will be able to see pretty well. At three weeks, the puppy can hear. Getting around is still a bit of a challenge for the little pups, but this skill is something these puppies will conquer quickly.

During the early weeks, the Boxer puppy begins to learn what it's like to be a dog. By being around its littermates and mother, it learns the rules and limits of play. Puppies that are removed from their litters too soon—before they are seven weeks old—will suffer mentally and, as a result, it can be difficult for an owner to overcome these handicaps even with extensive training. Studies indicate that puppies that are removed from their mothers and littermates at six weeks are not submissive to adult dogs, a dangerous thing for a puppy. Puppies separated at an early age also show abnormal behavior as adults in other studies. Though puppies are commonly sold at eight weeks of age, many breeders will not release their puppies until they are ten or twelve weeks old to assure the puppy has received the socialization it needs to begin its life.

This is also a critical time for the puppy to learn about humans. Experienced breeders gently handle their puppies throughout the day to begin and reinforce their trust in humans. Some research indicates that daily handling and picking up of puppies actually works toward inhibiting dominance aggression. Other studies indicate that regular handling of

These young puppies require feeding every few hours and stay together to keep warm.

young puppies may repress tendencies toward predatory behavior. The influence of handling during these early months is not totally known, but without a doubt, frequent handling and affection from humans helps Boxer puppies begin their development toward becoming loving canine companions.

During a puppy's first three months, it is critical to expose the puppy to as many friendly people as possible. Lack of human contact beyond the owner often creates unnecessary fear, wariness, and even phobias of people. The puppy should be introduced to all types of people, of all ages, and in a variety of settings, so that it doesn't fear a particular segment of the population, such as men, children, or people in uniform. This job begins with the breeder, and depending on when you bring home your new Boxer puppy, as much as a month of this early socialization period is in your hands.

Contact with Other Dogs

Socialization with friendly, well-trained, and vaccinated dogs is also important while your Boxer puppy develops. Contact with unvaccinated and potentially sick dogs should be avoided. Remember that your puppy has not been vaccinated enough at this point to prevent it from contracting a deadly virus. Don't risk the health of your puppy. If you know of a healthy, even-tempered dog that is up to date on its shots, then some play-

time for your puppy would be good. Once your veterinarian feels that your puppy has been properly vaccinated (between 12 and 16 weeks) and that it is not at risk among other dogs, you can begin puppy preschool classes where your puppy will be able to interact with several other puppies in a safe, controlled environment.

The first few months are not easy with a puppy, but they are rewarding. If you've done your job right, you will be well on your way to achieving a devoted, intelligent, and entertaining canine companion.

The Middle-aged Puppy: Four to Eight Months

When a puppy nears 16 weeks, an amazing thing happens—bladder control! This is exciting news for puppy parents who anxiously are awaiting more control from their puppy just as parents anxiously await giving up diapers. Now, this doesn't mean that a four-month-old puppy won't have any more accidents, and it doesn't mean you can trust it on the carpet. What it does mean is that your puppy may not dribble across the floor when it becomes excited. It may also be able to sleep comfortably for eight hours without having to get you up for a 2:00 A.M. relief walk. In many ways, this age marks the beginning of a puppy that is truly growing up.

Boxers love to chew, so make sure that you have plenty of toys on hand.

On the bad side, along with a gain in bodily function control also comes a loss of the puppy's milk teeth and the emergence of new adult teeth.

Teething Terror

There is probably nothing that will prepare you for this stage. Boxers are big chewers anyway, and the annoyance of new teeth coming in makes them, well, chewier.

• Make sure you have plenty of safe, indestructible chew toys for your dog.

• Discourage inappropriate chewing by not allowing anything within your puppy's reach that you don't want shredded or eaten.

• For those inanimate objects that you can't remove from your Boxer's chewing path but still can't stand to see destroyed, such as the cabinet corners or doors in the kitchen, or a table leg or two, spray or apply a harmless but foul-tasting formula specifically designed to discourage puppy chewing. Pet stores stock a variety of such products, as does your veterinarian.

Toys

"I want it! I want it!" No, that's not a toddler in the aisle of a toy store; it's your Boxer puppy begging for more stuff. Can you spoil a puppy with too many chew toys? Are you overindulging it if its toy basket runneth over? A resounding "No!" Some behaviorists recommend that you buy at *least* 15 indestructible toys for your puppy. Keep 10 out at all times, but rotate which toys you "hide" each day. With an ever-changing supply of toys to play with, your Boxer will be less likely to grow bored.

However, not all dog toys are created equally, and not all are safe for the mighty jaws of a growing Boxer puppy. When looking for suitable toys, here are a few things to consider:

Rotate your puppy's toys so that your Boxer doesn't grow bored.

• Balls can be swallowed. Buy only those that are too big to fit in your dog's mouth. Watch as your puppy grows, too. Balls that were too big to swallow last week may choke your Boxer this week.
• Look for breakable parts. Chew toys should not break off into pieces—ever.
• Avoid toys designed for small breeds. Cute little toys that are soft and have squeakies are not meant for a dog that has the jaws to hold onto a man's arm and not let go. Puppies will quickly rip these apart, and then swallow the offending squeakie.
• Think twice about pull toys. OK, you've got a dog that can hold a pull toy and win when it is just a few months old. Do you buy this toy? Do you engage in pulling games with your dog? Some trainers argue that this type of play encourages dominance aggression in dogs. Does it? Others say tug games are OK if the owner always wins. Perhaps the best advice is to hold off playing tug games until your dominance has been firmly and permanently established.

Training

Training a puppy that is four to eight months old is not difficult if the puppy has already been receiving training since it was very young (8 to 10 weeks). In fact, some aspects of training can become easier because the puppy is more mature and its attention span is longer. An unruly puppy at this age—one that has received no training—can be a handful, but don't despair. It is still very trainable and within a matter of a few weeks, it will be recognizing several commands.

The puppy's socialization with humans and dogs should not stop and owners should continue to introduce their Boxers to as many people and "things" as possible, using the *sit-stay* (see page 163) and having strangers offer the Boxer treats. Owners who have no young children or who live alone should seek out children. A Boxer lives up to its reputation of being good with children only if it is exposed to them constantly in a positive way. Make sure your Boxer is a role model.

Problems in socializing: If you are socializing your dog well and are actively enrolled in training classes, you should have few problems with your Boxer, but not all Boxers are perfect, and not all trainers are qualified to counsel owners who have dogs with behavior problems. You may need to seek the additional advice of a certified expert, such as a veterinary behaviorist or an applied animal behaviorist. The following are some red flags to watch out for with your growing puppy and are reasons to seek help immediately to prevent a more serious confrontation.
• Growling, snarling, or barking at all new dogs
• Barking, growling, or cowering at strangers (humans)
• Snarling or baring teeth when given a command or when touched or held by the collar

• Aggression toward other family pets, including other dogs and cats

The Adolescent Boxer: After Eight Months

Beginning at the age of eight months, your Boxer puppy will enter its "teen" years. Basically, this means you will have an adult-sized Boxer with a puppy's energy level that is beginning to experience a wide range of hormonal urges. That high-energy puppy that ricocheted off your walls for the past few months will still have a tremendous activity level, but now it will weigh up to 40 or 50 pounds (18–23 kg) *and* it will be gaining muscle bulk daily.

In other words, you'll have your hands full. Remember all that training you've done for the last six months? Be prepared for your adolescent Boxer to suddenly find ways to "untrain" itself. Watch out for stubborn streaks. And, keep your eyes open for attempts to reestablish the order and rank within your canine (and sometimes human) household. This is not to say that your Boxer will suddenly become vicious when it becomes an adolescent; it just is a warning that you'll need to keep up the good work with your Boxer and continue to mold it into a good canine companion.

If you haven't trained your Boxer consistently by the time it reaches adolescence, what are you waiting

Your Boxer puppy has a strong desire to please you.

for? It won't get easier. *Do it now.* The number one reason dogs are turned into the shelter is because their owners didn't take the time to train them. A trained Boxer is a joy to live with. An untrained *adolescent* Boxer is out of control. This is a very happy breed with lots of love and enthusiasm for everyone, but if you can't contain your Boxer, it may frighten or hurt someone with its sheer enthusiasm. This is not a tall dog but it is a strong dog. If you aren't experienced training Boxers, or if you are particularly small or not very strong, you may want to consider hiring a trainer to get your

Boxer going in the basics and then training *you* what he or she trained your dog. Once your Boxer learns the basics, you'll breathe a big sigh of relief.

Note: Boxers are an active breed, particularly as puppies; however, they are by no means "hyper." A hyperactive dog is one that is so frenzied that it *cannot* focus for any length of time. Training the hyper dog is frustrating if not impossible. The Boxer, on the other hand, may be *active,* but it has the mental capacity to focus on what you are teaching it. It also has the desire to please you.

Spay or Neuter

Something you will need to consider when your Boxer reaches adolescence—or before—is the decision to spay or neuter your dog. Unless you intend to be involved in showing or performance events and want to eventually breed your Boxer, it is in the Boxer's best interest, and yours, to have this surgery performed.

Males: A problem that compounds the Boxer's teen years is the surge of hormones that can course through a young male's body. Unless you are active in showing and might consider breeding your Boxer at a later date, your Boxer should be neutered by the time it reaches six months. Some recent studies indicate the procedure may be performed as early as eight weeks. Consult with your veterinarian for up-to-date information. An intact male can be a challenge to own. If there is a female within a mile that is in season, your wannabe stud will climb any fence and dig any hole to get to her, resulting in a litter of unwanted puppies. An intact male also can be much more aggressive with other dogs than a neutered male.

If you own a Boxer as a pet, or if you purchased a dog for showing or performance events that didn't quite measure up or has some hereditary defects or diseases, neuter your dog. You'll save yourself a lot of headaches and you'll decrease the risk of certain cancers for your dog. Neutering will *not* make your male Boxer a wimp, nor will the dog hold this procedure against you.

Fact

Of the dogs that have been killed by cars, as many as 85 percent are intact (unneutered) male dogs.

Females: An unspayed female will attract every male in the area when she comes in season. A female that is in season can also provoke terrible battles between unneutered male dogs that see themselves as possible suitors. She also has a hard time keeping herself clean during this time and can be a mess to clean up after around the house.

By spaying your female Boxer, you will spare yourself the headache of her coming into season. You may also very well extend the life of your female if you have her spayed as uterine cancers can be avoided, as well as other female reproductive diseases. Mammary cancer is also reported to be lower in spayed females if the surgical alteration is performed before the dog's first heat cycle.

Spaying and neutering are one-time procedures. They are performed so routinely by veterinarians across the country that owners should have few qualms if any about electing to have their pet altered.

All Grown Up

Most Boxers reach their full maturity by 18 months, some perhaps are late bloomers at two years. With the proper preventive veterinary care, a sound diet, plenty of socialization, consistent training, and lots of love, your Boxer should develop into the outstanding companion it was bred to be.

The Silver Boxer

As much as we wish our devoted Boxers could live forever, they don't. In fact, a Boxer that has reached its seventh birthday is considered a geriatric—or a silver Boxer. (Silver is in reference to the silver or white hairs that grow in around the Boxer's muzzle and eyes.)

With the aging process also come several changes in the Boxer itself. Owners who want to keep their older Boxers healthy and comfortable for as long as possible are advised to keep an eye on the following life changes in their dogs.

By the time your Boxer is seven or eight years old, you can expect to see a lot of white hairs throughout the dog's coat, giving your Boxer a silver appearance.

Lower Activity Level

For those owners who have been wishing that their active Boxer would just slow down, this is the time. Even if you don't wish your Boxer would become less active, it usually will. Without any other changes than activity level, however, your Boxer will gain weight and may become a rotund couch potato. Excessive weight at any age is not good, but with a senior, those extra pounds can place increased stress on the dog's heart and joints. In other words, a lot of fat is not good—for dogs or humans!

To prevent this from happening to your aging Boxer, there are several approaches that can be taken. One is to exercise your dog. When you no longer have a bouncy Boxer *begging* you to take it for a walk, many times owners *don't* take their dogs on walks. Make sure you can motivate your senior Boxer to exercise. Walks are always good, as are "self starters," those Boxers that will take any excuse they can think of to play. Often, a playful dog will get an older curmudgeon to play. If not, better beat the pavement with your Boxer— it's good for you, too. Keep the exercise fun and gentle, and at a pace your older Boxer can enjoy.

Another approach is to cut back on your dog's food. Feed your dog only enough food to provide all the necessary nutrients and keep the right amount of weight on it. If you can't stand those pleading eyes after you've fed your pet and it has licked the bowl clean from its smaller por-

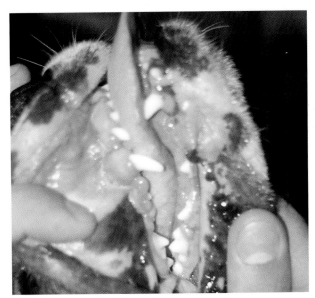

One condition that afflicts older Boxers is gingivival hyperplasia. Regular brushing is extremely important with this disease.

tions, ask your veterinarian if a special diet designed for seniors might be more appropriate for your Boxer. A senior diet should be highly palatable (taste good) and be highly digestible. Some dogs have difficulties digesting their food when they age and don't absorb all the necessary nutrients. If the food is easily digested, your Boxer has a greater chance to absorb the things it needs.

Perhaps, however, the best approach is to use both methods: gentle exercise and a reduced diet. Before you begin any weight reduction program with your Boxer, consult your veterinarian. There are other conditions, such as hypothyroidism, that can cause a significant weight gain.

Your aging Boxer may need special help to make its last few years comfortable.

Degenerative Diseases

Along with old age come a variety of diseases. Arthritis is common among aging Boxers and can have numerous causes. The end result, however, is a dog with swollen and painful joints. There are many traditional and holistic treatments for arthritis that can range in moderate to excellent pain reduction in your dog. Be sure to consult with your veterinarian for methods of treating this disease.

Eye ulcers (see "corneal ulcers," page 154) are another disease of aging Boxers that tends to strike female, spayed Boxers over the age of five. There are emerging methods for treating this disease if it is caught early enough.

Cancers are serious and this is the age group that is most often struck. Make it a regular part of your routine to brush your Boxer every day and rub your hands over the dog's entire body. *Any* lump or bump should be taken seriously and requires an immediate visit to your veterinarian.

Gingivival hyperplasia is a disease in which a dog's gums grow over its teeth. Geriatric Boxers suffer from this disease; therefore, it is critical that you brush your silver Boxer's teeth routinely—every day if possible—to prevent infections, abcesses, and just plain bad breath.

Incontinence

This is a topic that is taboo in human conversation and isn't really a hot topic among dog owners either, *but it does happen to many older dogs.* The first issue to be settled when you notice your dog having accidents is that the problem is incontinence and isn't something else, such as a bladder infection or some other illness.

If the incontinence stems from something that is not curable or treatable with medications developed to control this problem, the owner need only show some compassion and creativity to make the Boxer's life continue to be pleasant. One way to help your Boxer with its incontinence is to very closely monitor its eating and drinking and develop a schedule. As with a puppy, if you give your adult enough opportunities to relieve itself throughout its waking hours, it will have less opportunity to have an accident.

Another option you might consider is installing a dog door so the dog can go in and out at will to relieve itself. If the dog simply doesn't realize it has to go until it has gone (while it is sleeping at night, for example) consider purchasing a special bed for incontinent dogs. The pad is made of a fabric that wicks moisture away from the dog. Other beds are constructed with a mesh tray so that the dog can sleep on the tray and allow liquids to drain away from it.

When to Let Go

Unless your aging Boxer passes away quietly in its sleep, you will most likely be faced with a decision that only you can make: Is your dog so ill that it should be euthanized? The answer to this question should lie exclusively in your dog. In terminal cases, a dog should never have to suffer. If the dog's pain is liveable—by its standards, not yours—then there's no reason to worry about euthanasia at this point. If, however, the dog is in chronic pain and there is no cure, you need to put aside your feelings as best you can and consider your dog's situation. If there ever was a dog that could understand and even thank you for removing it from its suffering, it is the Boxer. Discuss the problem with your veterinarian.

No one knows the future of any Boxer and an owner can only hope that his or her Boxer will live a full and healthy life. Given the unknowns in life, it is best never to take any Boxer for granted. Learn to treasure every day you are blessed with owning such a very special dog.

Chapter Eight
Welcome Home!

Welcoming Puppies

Typically, most puppies are brought home at the age of eight weeks or so. The minute you pick up your Boxer puppy, you have taken on a serious responsibility. Separated from its mother, littermates, and the breeder, the puppy is completely dependent on you. You are now the puppy's mother, teacher, and human partner. It cannot survive or thrive without your help.

Fortunately, Boxers are very forgiving of their owners' mistakes, but for the welfare of your Boxer, it's helpful to understand how to care for your puppy, and to understand what those first few days and weeks home will be like.

The First Day

If you've done your homework, your Boxer is coming from a reputable breeder who is scrupulous about breeding for health, conformation, and temperament. Your Boxer puppy is up to date on its vaccinations, it has been wormed appropriately, and its coat is clean and free of fleas and ticks. It is all ready to go home.

Did you remember to make an appointment with your veterinarian? As mentioned earlier in this book, the best plan of action is to drive from the breeder's home to the veterinarian's office for both health and temperament evaluations. If this isn't possible—perhaps, you're traveling a long distance or it's a Sunday—make sure you get your puppy in to see your veterinarian as soon as possible, within three days *at the most*. If your puppy appears to be ill before your scheduled appointment, don't hesitate to call your veterinarian or, if it's after hours when you notice something is wrong, go to the emergency veterinary clinic in your area. Sick puppies can deteriorate rapidly, turning from a little sick to deathly ill in a matter of a day or less. Don't chance it. Get any illness checked out.

When you pick up your puppy it will be fully weaned from its mother. Just because the puppy does not depend on Mom for its meals, however, doesn't mean that it doesn't still depend on her in other ways. Your Boxer puppy will miss its mother the minute you walk out the breeder's door. The puppy will also

Bring your new puppy to the veterinarian as soon as possible.

miss its littermates that have been its constant playmates for the past several weeks or months. For the most part, until you walked into the picture, the Boxer puppy's mother and its littermates were this puppy's entire world. That tumbling mass of Boxer puppies are the canines that your puppy ate with, played with, and slept with to keep warm. Now all your puppy has is you.

Making the First Night Easier

No matter how great a Boxer owner you are or are going to be, you aren't going to be a suitable replacement for your puppy's mother and littermates—at first. With some exceptions, you can expect the typi-

cal Boxer puppy to cry, whimper, bark, and even howl a bit the first few days—especially when it is left alone.

However, there are things you can do to help gain a little sleep those first few nights and help your puppy make the transformation to its home life a little quicker.

1. One way is to make the puppy feel at home with something that smells familiar. Your young puppy has a very strong sense of smell and certain scents are very comforting to it. Several days before you go to pick up your puppy, give the breeder a towel or cuddly dog toy and ask him or her if they would "scent" the article for you. It takes only a short time of lying on the item by the puppy's mother to embed her scent into the item. Then, when you pick up your puppy to bring it home, you can take this scented item home, too. Having the mother's scent close to the puppy can be extremely comforting and can make for a quieter first few nights.

2. Another trick some puppy owners have used successfully is wrapping a sturdy clock in a sock or several socks. Some say the ticking

The sights and sounds of your neighborhood should be introduced to your Boxer pup in a positive way.

mimics the mother's heartbeat and helps to comfort the puppy that sorely misses its dog family. Some puppy owners will even wrap a warm water bottle in blankets to simulate the warmth of lying on a pile of puppies or "Mom." The sound of the television or a radio can also help relieve some of the puppy's distress.

3. Choosing the right type of crate to house your puppy can also affect the comfort of the puppy (see page 79). Many Boxers prefer the hard shell, "denlike" crate. The reason for this is that some dogs feel vulnerable in a wire crate because it is so open. Wrapping a wire crate in a heavy blanket to give it that "den" quality may help; your puppy may also discover what fun it is to pull the blanket into the crate to eat, too.

In the excitement of bringing home your puppy, be sure to allow the Boxer to sleep. Little puppies play hard and they need to sleep hard, too. Feed your young charge on a regular schedule (see Nutrition, page 126), and be sure that it does not have to compete for food with other family pets. Also, limit your puppy's exposure to unknown dogs. If you're not sure of the dog's vaccination history, it is better to limit your puppy's exposure until it is fully vaccinated.

The Following Week

After the first week you will begin to notice that life with your Boxer puppy is beginning to get more predictable, if not easier. Don't expect miracles in the house-training department, but your puppy may begin to "hold it" for six hours or so during the night, or at least alert you when it needs to relieve itself.

This is the time period—after the dust has settled from the puppy's first week—when the owner can now begin taking more time to meet the puppy's developmental needs. As previously discussed, this is a critical period for your puppy's socialization. This is when you begin introducing your Boxer puppy to everyone and everything in a controlled manner. You want the people your Boxer meets to be friendly and gentle. You want the dogs it meets to be friendly and gentle, too, and fully vaccinated. And finally, you want the sights and sounds of your neighborhood to be introduced to your puppy in a positive and reinforcing manner. In other words, if a fire engine roars down your street, allow your puppy to be interested, but don't drag it to the street corner to get a better look. Let your puppy take little steps forward and always keep its training positive and consistent.

The Months Ahead

Speaking of training, the moment your puppy enters your home you should be involved in training it. Whether you realize it or not, everything you do or say around your puppy is part of your puppy's training. For this reason, it is wise to really read up on teaching young puppies so that you won't inadvertently teach your puppy the wrong behaviors. In other words, when your puppy smells dinner being set on the table and it runs over, tries to jump on the chair, and starts barking, what it learns at this point is entirely dependent on your reaction. Do you look lovingly at the puppy and say, "Oh you cute, sweet thing, here's a little treat for you," thereby encouraging future behavior when the dog is 60 pounds (27 kg) and capable of jumping on the table and stealing your entire meal, or do you gently pull your puppy from the chair, remove it from the dinner situation, and then put it in a *sit-stay*—rewarding this final behavior with a doggie treat?

Though the example above seems very obvious when written down in black and white, it's not so clear-cut in our day-to-day choices with puppies. Puppies are very cute when they jump up and try to lick us in friendly greetings, but is this the behavior you want your full-grown Boxer to have when your frail Aunt Myrna comes to visit? What about barking? Puppies can be very vocal, but do you want to encourage this behavior in the adult? One owner thought it was so cute when her puppy was growling and barking at the other puppies. Wrong! Dog-dog aggression is not cute and should never be encouraged. But when the owner's response to this aggression was positive, the unwanted behavior was reinforced.

So, as a new owner, be sure to consider how you respond to your Boxer puppy's behaviors. In these first few months every action counts and it is often much harder if not impossible to "undo" a dog's behavior than it is to prevent the incident from ever occurring in the first place.

Friendship Is a Treat Away

A good way to introduce your puppy to new people is to put it in a *sit* (see page 162). Hand the "stranger" a small bit of treat, and ask him or her to feed it to your puppy. Your puppy will quickly realize that if it is good and sits nicely, it will be richly rewarded. Your neighbors will appreciate the dedication with which you are training your Boxer and will be much more receptive to you and your dog when your puppy reaches its full size. As Boxer owners know, these dogs are pretty much big marshmallows at heart; however, most onlookers are extremely intimidated by the Boxer's strength and powerful bite. Having introduced your puppy in its lovable stage and reinforcing this friendly behavior with treats goes a long way toward establishing good neighbor relations.

If your puppy is particularly wary of strangers and won't sit still to allow them to feed it a snack—or if your dog shows *any* signs of aggression such as growling or raised fur on the neck—get to a respected trainer immediately. Aggression and fearfulness in many cases can be tackled and overcome when the Boxer is a puppy. The longer this behavior goes uncorrected, however, the more difficult it becomes to correct.

Learning your lifestyle: For the first month your puppy is home, it is also important to introduce it to your lifestyle. You'll want to take the puppy on frequent rides in the car. If you are using a crate in your home, make sure your puppy is comfortable with its new home. Do the garbage trucks come on Thursday mornings? Make sure your Boxer is able to see the trucks and is rewarded for good behavior. Steps in the house, toilets flushing, and vacuum cleaners running are other situations that you will want your Boxer to be comfortable with and not to fear.

To reinforce positive reactions to these "stimuli," behaviorists recommend catching the puppy when it responds appropriately, without fear or aggression, and rewarding that behavior with a treat. "Coddling" a puppy when it shows fear only reinforces this behavior; in effect, the attention is rewarding the puppy for showing its fearfulness. So, if your puppy responds to a bicyclist going down the street by tucking its tail (what it has of a tail) and trying to duck away, don't pick it up and say, "Oh, you'll be OK, sweetie." Instead, ignore the puppy's behavior. Distract it to look at something else and reward it for calm behavior.

Finally, studies show that "enriched" puppies that have had a multitude of positive experiences during their first 12 weeks are generally less fearful and are more likely to be emotionally balanced than older puppies with fewer experiences. So the word is, get out there and introduce your puppy to the world. Keep the experience positive. Reward for good behavior. Your efforts will be rewarded tenfold in the future with a well-adjusted, social Boxer.

What to Watch Out For

The following traits are considered common dog behaviors, but they are undesirable and should be dealt with in a gentle, consistent manner to prevent these behaviors from becoming part of a puppy's regular behavior. For up-to-date methods of discouraging these behaviors, consult a skilled trainer, an accredited animal behaviorist, or a knowledgeable veterinarian for advice.
• A puppy that growls while eating or while chewing bones; this could be a sign of territorial aggression or dominance aggression.
• A puppy that struggles hard or even bites when held; this puppy could challenge its human owners for the "alpha" position at a later time.
• A puppy that repeatedly nips children or adults; a puppy often views children as playmates or other puppies.

Welcoming the Rescued Boxer

Some rescued Boxers walk into a home, take a look around, and settle in as if they have lived there all their lives. They're house-trained, have nice manners, and know several helpful commands. Sound like a dream? OK, in many instances it is. Remember the primary reason dogs are given up to shelters? *They are not trained.* They are good dogs that have been allowed to behave badly.

The problems of rescued Boxers, however, are rarely insurmountable. If they were, a responsible rescue would not be placing the dog. And, for a person with prior Boxer experience, transitioning an adult Boxer into a new home may seem quite simple. For the inexperienced Boxer owner, there are a few "adopted" dog tips you should consider.

The First Day

Bringing home an adopted Boxer can be every bit as exciting as bringing home a new puppy. It can also be just as exhausting. Here are a few ideas as to what you can expect and how you can make this day less stressful.

1. First, before you leave to pick up your adopted Boxer, have your home ready. Read through the chapter Preparing for the New Arrival, page 75, and prepare yourself well. With a puppy, you may have a couple of days grace period before the real destruction kicks in. With an adult dog, there is no grace period. If you don't want your dog in carpeted areas at first—a good idea—then make these areas inaccessible. If your gate to the backyard doesn't shut all the way, fix it now. And, be sure to purchase a sturdy dog crate that will fit your new Boxer. Your adoption agency should be able to give you an exact size based on the dog's height and length.

2. When you go to pick up your Boxer, take the crate in your car. When transporting your Boxer home from the rescue or adoption facility, you should use a crate. There are several reasons for this. The first is that you do not know this dog yet. If it panics when a motorcycle guns past your car, you could end up with a full-grown Boxer trying to crawl into your lap while you barrel down the highway at 65 miles (105 km) an hour. It is safer for both you and your new dog if your dog rides in either a travel crate or a partitioned section of your vehicle.

Boxer rescue will help to find the right Boxer for the right family.

The second reason for restraining—we won't say "caging"—your Boxer during its first ride with you is that this literally could be one of its *very first* car rides. A nervous Boxer may drool profusely, shake, pace, throw up, or relieve itself. Also, a shelter Boxer may be infested with fleas or ticks or be suffering from a parasitic infection (worms, giardia). If the dog is crated, the damage is minimal. If the dog is loose, well, at a minimum you'll have a mess. If the dog is suffering from something more serious, you may suffer more serious consequences, too.

3. Next, make sure you take your Boxer directly to your veterinarian for a complete health and temperament evaluation. If you adopted your Boxer from a breed rescue, these services may have already been performed. If your Boxer tested negative on its heartworm test and is on preventive medicine, fine, you don't need to have this tested again. Likewise, if the dog has verification of all its vaccinations, there's no need to repeat these. However, have your veterinarian evaluate your Boxer's temperament. Though the Boxer is renowned and treasured for its even, loving temperament, and has been known to endure past lives in abusive situations and still maintain this inherent temperament, it is always a wise move to have the dog evaluated carefully. This evaluation is particularly important if you are adopting the Boxer from a facility that does not offer this service. It is equally wise to have your veterinarian evaluate your Boxer, even when you have adopted it from a reputable breed rescue or a breeder. A second opinion can be invaluable. The veterinarian may just pick up on some quirk that eluded the foster "parents" of the dog. Do it.

4. If your dog is coming from a shelter and has not been bathed, groomed, or dipped, make sure your next appointment is with the groomer. This has been mentioned previously in this book, but it really bears repeating: Don't bring home a dirty, infested dog. Why subject your other pets or yourself to something you don't have to? The grooming fee for bathing, dipping, if necessary, and drying a Boxer is not substantial and it will make your first day a bit easier. The only exception to this suggestion is a case in which the nerves of the adopted Boxer may not quite be up to the hustle and bustle of the grooming shop. If this describes your Boxer, you may have to be a little more careful and enlist the help and expertise of a more experienced Boxer owner.

5. Once your adult Boxer is home, you'll want to walk it right away upon exiting the car. Resist the temptation to immediately bring it into your home or parade it past the neighbors. There'll be plenty of time for that later. To help begin house-training, or to reinforce the training the Boxer already has, try to have it relieve itself in its new yard. Unless the Boxer has worms or is being wormed, don't be in a hurry to "pick up" quite yet. You'll want to leave a

Rescued Boxers come in all shapes and sizes.

scent in the yard so that your Boxer knows this area is OK (for more on house-training, see page 167).

6. Once your Boxer has done its outdoor duties, then you can bring your new dog into the home. Again, resist taking your Boxer places it won't be allowed to go initially. Keep the Boxer in its area. Show it where its bed or crate will be. Give it some fresh cool water. Bring out a few interesting dog toys and a safe chew bone. Speak gently with your new adult and offer it a few handheld treats. Your Boxer will be very curious and you can expect it to check out its area and you quite thoroughly.

How long it takes for your dog to begin showing signs of relaxing in your home really depends on the individual dog. Some rescued adults walk into a house, find the softest place they're allowed to lie on, and crash from their hectic first day. Others may trot around the house and yard for an hour or more. Be sure to allow your Boxer to relieve itself frequently—either by walks or in the yard—to avoid any nervous mistakes in your home. To avoid a potential bout with bloat (see page 147), make sure your Boxer has settled down comfortably before you feed it a meal. If your Boxer is uneasy throughout the day, you may want to hand-feed it bits of food at a time.

Adopting an adult dog enables the prospective owner to take much of the guesswork out of dog ownership.

The First Night

When it comes time to settle down for the night, walk your Boxer one more time, allowing it to relieve itself. Then, put it in its crate, which should be lined with a comfortable, washable blanket or soft cover. Then brace yourself. If you thought a puppy was noisy when left alone its first night, you'll be impressed with the sounds and noises that can come from an adult Boxer. The adult Boxer obviously is not troubled with a puppy's pangs of leaving its litter-mates and mother; however, it could be uncomfortable with a change in lifestyle, even though this new lifestyle is in most cases significantly better than what it was used to.

In basic terms, some adopted dogs simply handle change better than others. On the first night in a new home, some adult Boxers will put their heads down and immediately go to sleep in the comfort and safety of their crate, seemingly appreciative of everything you've done for them. Other adult Boxers are less than thrilled with a different routine and are more likely to vocalize on their uncertainty.

What do you do? You can put a particularly attractive chew toy or bone in the Boxer's crate to help keep its mind off the separation. You can also visit the Boxer at intervals to reassure it and talk to it. Some owners put the Boxer's crate where it can see them sleeping and gradually move the crate to another area.

For the most part, the adult Boxer will adjust very quickly to its new

Though rescued Boxers are usually quite content to be favored pets, they are working dogs at heart and enjoy being trained for a variety of sports.

surroundings and will not keep its new owners awake for very many nights. Since it has excellent control over its bodily functions, it also will be able to sleep through the night—assuming it is fed on a schedule that permits this.

Getting to Know Each Other

Often, the only information that a rescue or adoption facility has on a Boxer is their observations about how the Boxer has behaved while under *their* care. Little is known about the Boxer's past. Was it socialized with other pets? Is it tolerant of children? Will it jump fences or dig holes? Is it terrorized by thunder? Does it have any phobias?

The first month or two of owning an adopted Boxer is a learning period for both dog and human. During this time, your Boxer very well may behave like a big puppy, investigating every aspect of your home with wonder and true Boxer amazement. A flushing toilet may invoke a playful response. In some instances, the same stimulus may evoke an apprehensive or even fearful response in a less confident dog. Your Boxer may never have seen a screen before and might charge through your door, ripping down and shredding a lightweight screen. Glass windows may not be recognized as being solid; be sure to introduce your Boxer to the windows just to make sure this isn't the case.

If your Boxer was mistreated, it will also be a time for it to learn to trust humans again. Kindness, patience, and love work wonders. Sometimes you may discover something in your home that elicits a fearful response from your Boxer. You will need to work toward conditioning your dog to overcome its fears. Generally, this involves ignoring fearful responses and rewarding positive behaviors. A good trainer should be able to help you and your dog work through a variety of problems—which leads to the next point: Begin training your Boxer immediately.

Training

Even if your Boxer comes to you well trained or trained enough to navigate effectively through day-to-day living, you still need to take it through basic obedience. Training your dog and working on commands on a daily basis will help establish a strong bond between you and your dog. It also helps to enforce who is the leader in the relationship. Of course, another major benefit to taking your dog to training classes is that you have a wonderful contact for advice on problems. An experienced and reputable trainer is a real treasure to know. Cultivate this contact and do not hesitate to consult with your trainer for any behavioral dilemmas. You also can always contact your breed rescue person for advice and tips.

Above all, with an adopted Boxer the rule is to *take things slowly.* Do not expect too much from your adopted Boxer too soon. Remember, whether they are baby steps or giant leaps, any progress in the right direction is still progress. Most adult Boxers will adjust quickly to their new homes, but it's far better to make this adjustment safely and lovingly than to rush a dog. Your newly adopted Boxer will gladly give you its entire life to share if you just take the time to ease it into your life. You'll be glad you took the time.

The Rescued Boxer as a Second Dog

Owning Boxers can become addictive and sometimes just one Boxer isn't enough. (Two Boxers can have such great fun together!) Many times, Boxer owners choose to rescue an adult Boxer as their second dog. To add a second dog to the family, both the dog selection and the initial introduction of the two dogs is critical to making the relationship work. As mentioned before, if a Boxer holds a grudge against another Boxer, the two may have to be separated for life. The key is to never allow the grudge to happen in the first place.

Dog Selection

When considering a second Boxer for your family, it is important to try to find a match that will cause the least amount of friction. Male-female pairings generally work best. If you have an adult male in the home, for example, choosing an adult female as the second dog will maximize your chances of the two getting along, or at least tolerating each other.

Same-sex pairings can be successful, too, but care needs to be given in determining the dominance of the dogs. A very dominant female will most likely butt heads with another dominant female and the same with males, whether or not they are neutered. Why? Because with two dominant animals there will be a struggle for control or "top dog." If the two can work it out without getting into a full-blown fight, a same-sex pairing can work. In other words, if the dogs accept their respective ranks and aren't constantly challenging each other to be "alpha," the two should live peacefully.

The Introduction

Much of how the resident Boxer will take to the new Boxer (and vice versa) depends on how they are introduced. Behaviorists recommend introducing the dogs *on leash* to each other and rewarding them with food treats if they are relaxed and behave themselves. The new dog should remain still, in a *sit-stay,* if necessary, while the resident dog is allowed to approach the stationary dog. Keep it happy and fun, rewarding both dogs with treats for not growling or snapping. Once the resident dog has had a chance to meet the new dog, switch places and repeat the exercise.

If all is going well, you can allow the dogs to check each other out while still on leash. Hopefully, they will already be excited about the opportunity to have a playmate and you will be well on your way to establishing a peaceful dog family. For the first few days and even weeks, it is advisable to separate the dogs when you can't watch them interacting together. Crating when you are away from home or when you are sleeping is a good idea.

If the dogs aren't progressing toward a friendship and if the new dog seems to be challenging the resident dog, your work toward getting the two to get along may be more difficult. The experts say there is more hope for solving aggression between two dogs in the same family than dogs of different owners; however, until the pecking order is *permanently* established, you may have some confrontations between the dogs. If the dogs simply can't work it out, you may have to keep them permanently separated.

The Boxer rescue you adopted your dog from will be able to give you additional advice. on helping dogs accept each other. In some cases, the rescue may suggest replacing the rescued Boxer with one that is less confrontational. Just as some people don't get along well with other people, some Boxers may require a single-dog home, but these dogs are generally the exception to the rule. Most Boxers, if paired well and introduced in a safe and calm manner, welcome the addition of another playmate.

Chapter Nine

Grooming and Feeding

Boxers are a joy to care for in the grooming and feeding department. After the initial time and expense that may be incurred if you choose to have a puppy's ears cropped, the Boxer is truly a low-maintenance breed. This is not to say, however, that the Boxer is a no-maintenance dog. If you want your canine to sport a glossy coat, have a sparkle in its eyes, and have physical strength and energy, you'll need to invest some effort into your Boxer's upkeep.

Brushing

Beginning with the basics, brushing a shorthaired breed such as the Boxer is relatively simple; perhaps *remembering* to brush your pet from time to time is actually the hard part. If you don't brush your Boxer's coat on a regular basis, it will shed. It's part of the natural process of being a dog. Old hair falls out; new hair grows in. The only bad part is that the dog hair laws read that white hairs invariably must fall on dark-colored upholstery and clothes, and dark hairs must lodge themselves

deeply into the only white chair in the house!

As for brushing, your Boxer will enjoy a daily brushing with a brush—soft natural or rubber bristles that will catch the hairs are fine—but once a week should suffice to keep too many hairs from dropping into your furniture.

Spring shedding is not a problem with this breed because the Boxer rarely has a winter coat to shed in the spring. For the most part, Boxers do not fare well in cold weather and much prefer the warmth of their human companion's home and hearth to the elements of the outside. Therefore, a well-kept Boxer will never develop any winter thickness to its coat because it simply isn't outside for any period of time. However, don't take this to mean that a Boxer could be kept outside and it would develop a thick coat. A thicker coat, perhaps, but nothing substantial enough to keep it warm in cold weather.

Brush Puppies Early

To make grooming a pleasurable experience for all, it is wise to begin brushing your puppy on a daily basis. Though your puppy may not need brushing this frequently, it is generally easier to get a small puppy to stand still for grooming than it is an older puppy that is untamed to the ways of the brush.

A good time to brush your puppy is after it has played hard and is almost ready to sleep. With the puppy relaxed and in your lap, you can gently begin stroking it. Older puppies can be put in a *stand-stay* and brushed in this manner. If you are planning on showing your Boxer, you will want to accustom it to a grooming table when it is young, too.

With puppies of any age, gently discourage any chewing of the brush; otherwise, when your Boxer is larger, you'll find yourself on the losing end of a tug-of-war battle.

Your Boxer will enjoy a daily brushing and rub down, which is easy to do with the Boxer's short coat.

Flea Combing

If you live in an area that has problems with fleas either in the summer or year-round, investing in a flea comb is not a bad idea. There are many different products on the market that help to control fleas (see Fleas, page 144); however, many don't kill adult fleas immediately. Also, many flea products are not approved for puppies younger than six months of age, which means if your puppy has fleas, you'll have to either shampoo frequently or use a flea comb, or both. With a flea comb, which is a metal comb with long, closely spaced teeth, you can pick adult fleas out of your Boxer's coat, but you won't be able to capture most of the eggs. If your Boxer has a flea allergy, keeping fleas off its skin can be the difference between your dog having a great summer and a miserable one.

Other than a regular brushing and checking for fleas and ticks during warmer months, there's really little else to do with your Boxer's coat other than to wash it from time to time.

Bathing

Unless your Boxer makes it a habit to tunnel through your flower beds on a regular basis, you really won't have to bathe it very often. Weekly brushing should be enough to keep your dog's skin healthy and to keep the shedding of hairs at a minimum. Bathing your Boxer is really only necessary when it has particularly dirtied itself or if it begins to smell a bit too doggy. Because shampooing a dog's coat tends to dry the skin somewhat and remove naturals oils from the dog's coat, frequent shampooing is not recommended. Again, with regular brushing, a Boxer really shouldn't need a bath more than once a month in the summer and perhaps once every two months in cooler weather.

When you do bathe your Boxer, use a shampoo that is formulated specifically for dogs. Human shampoos are designed for a different pH level and will dry a dog's skin. They may also irritate your Boxer's eyes. If your Boxer has dry skin or has skin allergies, be sure to consult with your veterinarian about specific shampoos that can be used to help rather than increase this problem.

When bathing your Boxer, consider your puppy or dog's comfort level. Only bathe your Boxer outdoors if the weather is warm. In winter months, use a tub indoors, or a dry shampoo that brushes in and brushes out. Also, if possible, use warm water when wetting and rinsing your Boxer. No dog enjoys icy water and puppies are particularly sensitive to cold water. Make the

bath enjoyable and healthy for your Boxer and there will be less of a struggle later.

Also, while bathing your dog, try to avoid getting water or soap in its eyes and ears. Soap can burn a dog's eyes. As for your dog's ears, it is important to minimize their contact with water because a dog's ears are constructed differently than a human's and do not naturally drain as well.

After your Boxer's bath is completed and you've thoroughly washed all the soap out of the puppy or dog's coat, you can towel-dry your dog. Make sure that your Boxer can finish its drying in a warm, comfortable place; this is not the time for cold drafts. Also, you may want to make sure your Boxer can't run free in the backyard when it is still damp dry. As soon as you let it out in the yard, it is sure to dig a hole or roll in a muddy patch. It's not that your Boxer is being spiteful; it's just that it feels so good. To keep yourself happy and your Boxer clean, try to keep the dog or puppy restrained until its coat has dried.

Clean It All

When bathing your dog, clean its bedding, too. There's nothing more disheartening than to have shampooed and washed your Boxer only to have it run over and rub itself all over its smelly old bed. Most beds have removable covers that can be washed. If you've had the inside padding for a while, you may want to replace that, too.

Ears

As mentioned earlier, a dog's ears should not be exposed to water or soap during a bath. So, how do you clean them? Unless your dog is troubled with ear infections, all you need to do is take a clean cotton ball and wipe as much of the ear as possible. *Do not use a cotton swab to reach the dog's ear canal.* This is very dangerous and unnecessary. Top authorities in the veterinary field relate that the once-popular practice of plucking hairs from a dog's ear canal is not necessary for most dogs, either. Basically, the advice is that a dog's ears should not be messed with unless there is a problem. Excessive plucking can cause irritation to the ear canal, which, in turn, makes it ripe for a bacterial or yeast infection.

It is advisable, however, to sniff your dog's ears frequently. An ear infection will have a very foul odor. There may also be a lot of discharge coming from your dog's ear or ears. If either symptom is present in your Boxer's ears, get it to the veterinarian immediately. Untreated outer ear infections can progress into a serious condition quickly.

Cropping

This surgical procedure is an elective procedure in the United States, but has been banned in England, Germany, Sweden, and several other European countries. As discussed in Chapter Two (Cropped Ears, page 21), the decision as to whether or not to crop ears is largely a cosmetic one and is up to the breeder or owner. The long, tapered cut that is popular in the show ring today, however, must be made when the puppy is 9 to 12 weeks. Waiting beyond this age to have the surgery performed is not advisable, according to experienced breeders. Trying to crop the ears of an older puppy makes it much more difficult, if not impossible to achieve nicely set cropped ears.

Because the surgery must be performed at such a tender age, if you do not want your puppy's ears cropped, it is critical that you inform your breeder immediately. Otherwise, you may come to pick up your puppy and find it in an ear rack.

If you've decided you want to have your puppy's ears cropped, the

Wipe your Boxer's ears with a cotton ball. If you notice an abnormal amount of secretions or a nasty smell, take your Boxer to the veterinarian immediately.

most important thing *you must* do is work with an experienced and talented ear-cropping veterinarian. It is illegal and extremely dangerous to have a layperson attempt to crop a Boxer's ears. Ear cropping is considered major surgery for a dog and requires that the dog be under general anesthesia for more than an hour. Make absolutely sure that you have this procedure performed by a skilled veterinarian.

Of course, you don't want just any veterinarian cropping ears. There is a true art to cutting the ear into a long show crop; an inexperienced or sloppy cropping job can ruin a Boxer's chances of ever doing well in the show ring. Therefore, seek out a highly qualified veterinarian who is strongly recommended by Boxer breeders in your area.

In addition to simply having a good eye, steady hands, and a knack for working with Boxer ears, the veterinary surgeon must take several factors into consideration when cropping a puppy's ears: the weight of the ear leather—thin ears will stand with higher points than a thicker, heavier ear flap—the shape of the puppy's ear cartilage, and the puppy's muscle control and age.

Postsurgical care: Once the ears are successfully cropped, the complete success of the ear crop now falls on the owner and his or her ability and commitment to carefully follow the veterinarian's postsurgical care instructions. If an owner is not committed to keeping the wounds clean (at least twice daily for four to five days), and visiting his or her veterinarian every two weeks for checking the ears' progress and retapings, an ear cropping can be a terrible mistake. The cut edges can become infected in the early stages and improper attention to subsequent taping can produce a dog with floppy rather than erect cropped ears. Working with the cropped ears until they are set properly and stand erect can take anywhere from 2 weeks to 24 weeks or more if there are difficulties.

If you are going to invest the time and money into cropped ears, invest it in an experienced, qualified veterinarian and be prepared to commit to months of biweekly visits to your veterinarian for retaping the dog's ears.

Do-it-yourselfers: There are books on the market and web sites on the Internet that show detailed methods of posting ears either with mole foam or the more traditional "plug and tape" techniques. Though these outlines are very descriptive and come from reliable, experienced sources, the reality of doing this job yourself is not discussed. Imagine trying to convince a wiggly Boxer puppy that it really does want a cardboard tampon applicator wrapped in sticky tape and taped into each ear. Or, picture attempting to remove mole foam that had been applied with surgical glue two weeks ago, and then convincing this same puppy that you're going to re-glue fresh mole foam to its ears for another week.

If you are a very experienced breeder, you may have done these procedures scores of times and feel very comfortable performing all of your puppy's postsurgical care yourself. You know the ins and outs, you know how to use olive oil or ointments when massaging the ears, and you know how to correct ears that are pitching inward. If you are new to the breed, however, or just don't want to bother with this by yourself, make sure you budget for the necessary veterinary visits. This is certainly not the time to try to save money. How you care for your Boxer's newly cropped ears in these first few months will affect how your Boxer looks for the remainder of its life.

Nail Care

Trimming your Boxer's toenails should be a regular part of your dog-grooming efforts. Some dogs' nails grow quickly; others seem to remain short for long periods of time. Whether your Boxer's nails grow quickly or more slowly, they should always be kept short. Long nails can cause a dog's toes to spread in awkward and uncomfortable positions. They also catch easier and can cause your dog to break a nail or pull the entire nail from the toe, both very painful.

Trimming nails is relatively easy if you begin conditioning your Boxer as a puppy. Wait until the puppy is tired after playing or eating. While it is lying down, gently hold each paw

and touch the nail trimmer to the puppy's toenails. Reward the puppy for its good behavior with a treat. Do this on a daily basis. When the puppy's nails have finally grown enough to actually trim—this may be a couple of weeks—you can clip the tips of the nails. Since the puppy is so small at this point, a regular toenail clipper will be too large to accurately clip the nails. Try using a clipper for toy breeds or even a cat's claw trimmer. These smaller nail trimmers are easier to maneuver with little nails. As your Boxer grows, you can purchase a larger nail trimmer.

How to trim: The most important part of clipping a dog's toenails is to avoid cutting into the "quick," or the nail's blood supply. If your Boxer has white paws, it will most likely

Grinding nails down eliminates sharp edges left by clipping that could catch on upholstery.

have clear nails on some, if not all of its toes. With a clear nail, it is very easy to see where the quick ends in the nail. Place the trimmers a smidge beyond the end of the quick, and trim quickly. If your Boxer has some black or dark nails, use the amount you trimmed from the clear nail as a guide for where to place the trimmer on these nails. If your Boxer has all dark nails, you will have to look more closely at the nail to find where the quick ends.

It is always a good idea to keep a towel nearby when trimming, in case you do quick the dog. Also, there are products on the market that promptly stop the bleeding of a quicked toenail; you should have it handy when you are trimming nails.

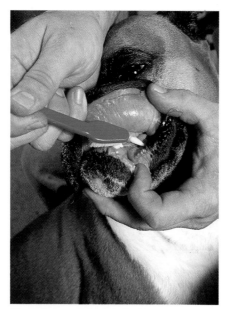

Brushing your Boxer's teeth on a regular basis prevents tooth decay and eliminates bad breath.

Another way to trim nails is with an electric grinder that grinds the nails to a smooth finish. It takes a little longer than clipping, and it makes more noise. It also vibrates slightly and the ground toenails do smell a bit, but if you get your Boxer used to this procedure, it can be an efficient way to trim nails. Many people use the grinder to smooth out their dog's toenails after they've been clipped.

If you can't clip your Boxer's toenails for some reason, make sure to take your dog to a groomer to have this done on a regular basis. Every month to six weeks should be sufficient, with some Boxers requiring less frequent visits.

Dental Care

Brush a Boxer's teeth? If this suggestion from your veterinarian takes you off guard, consider these recent statistics: Most dogs (85 percent) over the age of four have periodontal disease. They also have bad breath. Back in the old days of dog ownership, not much thought was given to a dog's teeth other than opting to feed dry food rather than moist and perhaps to keep good chew toys or bones available to the dog. The concept of taking a brush to a dog's teeth was totally foreign, except perhaps to exhibitors who worked to make every aspect of the Boxer as presentable as possible.

Of course, back in the old days, a lot of dogs had a lot fewer teeth.

To prevent bad breath, gum disease, tartar buildup, and tooth loss, the strong recommendation by the veterinary community is to get your puppy accustomed to having its teeth brushed at least one or more times a week. One of the easiest ways to begin this process is to use what is called a finger brush, a soft plastic, nubby cylinder that fits over your finger. Your puppy or adult is much less likely to balk at your fingers going in its mouth, especially when covered in a delectable chicken- or beef-flavored canine toothpaste, than it would be if you tried to use a dog toothbrush. The best time to attempt to introduce your Boxer to a tooth brushing is when it is tired and content. With regular practice, eventually you will be able to use a toothbrush.

Toothpaste for Dogs

You may be tempted to pull out your favorite toothpaste and use it on your dog in a pinch, but resist this temptation; the effects could be very detrimental. Toothpaste designed for humans should never be used on a dog's teeth. The ingredients in human products can be harmful to dogs if swallowed. Since it's impossible to teach a Boxer to spit, it's best to use products that are both effective in cleaning the dog's teeth and safe for a dog to swallow.

Rinsing and Flossing

If your dog has a serious problem with its teeth, your veterinarian may recommend that you add a dental rinse to your regular toothbrushing regime. The rinse is specifically designed for dogs and is safe for use. (Of course, your dog does not have to know how to gargle and spit!) The rinses generally come in a plastic bottle with a tip that allows you to squirt the fluid onto the dog's gum line.

As for flossing, there really isn't any dental floss made for dogs. There are some products available, however, including rope toys that when chewed simulate some of the motion of using dental floss. Beyond this, very determined owners can train their dogs at an early age to lie still, head in the owner's lap, while their teeth are being scaled. The tool used on a dog is very similar to that used on humans. It does have a very sharp point, so great care must be taken when scaling teeth not to scratch, cut, or tear the dog's gums.

Chew, Chew, Chew

If tooth decay is a problem with your Boxer, or if it has or is developing periodontal disease, you will want to take a close look at what you are feeding your dog in the way of snacks and meals. Semimoist and moist foods do not help diminish the tartar buildup in your dog's mouth, but hard kibble does. Some pet food manufacturers have even designed special foods for dogs with dental disease. These are generally larger and perhaps crunchier kibble that helps to remove the by-products of eating much as a good chew bone might.

The classic chew bone and chew toys should not be overlooked, either. Avoid chew bones that break down into a gummy mess and instead, choose products that give your Boxer the firmness and texture it needs to help it clean its teeth. Plastic bones impregnated with flavor can be a good choice, as can be some of the hard-baked bones that are hard out of the package but can be softened up to a dog biscuit texture in the microwave. There are so many innovative chew products on the market it won't take long to find one that your dog enjoys and will use.

Nutrition

Proper maintenance of your Boxer requires that you also feed it well. That does not mean to kill your dog with kindness and overfeed it. Feeding your dog well in this context means to meet your dog's nutritional requirements. A properly fed Boxer will have energy and a wonderfully glossy coat. It may also have less opportunity to develop certain diseases and disorders that are related to malnutrition or obesity.

Finding the best food for your Boxer, however, is not necessarily an easy task. One walk down the aisle of any pet store and an owner can quickly get confused about which food to choose. Reading the labels may not help much if you don't know what you're looking for, and just because a food is packaged attractively and is very expensive

doesn't mean your Boxer will thrive on it.

What you need to consider is how the food is packaged, what nutrients it includes, and for what life stage it was developed. The following is a brief nutrition primer that will help you make the right choice in selecting your dog's food.

Packaging

There are three basic ways dog foods are packaged: canned, semimoist, or dry. In some areas, you may be able to purchase meat-based products that are frozen.

Canned: Canned foods are mostly water (up to 75 percent or more) and are the most expensive of commercial dog foods. Though feeding canned foods may reduce your dog's risks of bloat as it doesn't expand in the stomach as dry kibble would, it is the most expensive option, especially when the dog is medium to large. Canned foods generally contain few preservatives because of the processes involved in the canning procedure, but they also contain a high percentage of fat. Because the food is soft, it does not provide your Boxer with any teeth-cleaning benefits.

Semimoist: Semimoist foods are high in sugars, can be expensive, and generally are not recommended for dogs by veterinarians.

Dry: Dry foods help to avoid tooth decay and are a better choice for a Boxer with dental problems than a soft or semimoist food. Dry foods contain the least amount of fat and

Meals should be fed at least twice a day using a good-quality food.

are economical to feed. On the flip side, dry foods have the greatest amount of preservatives among dog foods, and the dry food does expand in a dog's stomach, which may cause problems in a Boxer that is predisposed to or has a higher risk of developing bloat.

Frozen: Frozen dog foods are not widely available, but may show promise in providing dogs with a fresh, lower-cost option. Storage can be a problem with these foods, but if you're willing to invest in an outdoor garage freezer or forego your personal ice cream stash in the home, this may not be a problem.

Life Stages

In addition to developing several types of dog foods, manufacturers produce foods specifically created to meet the particular nutritional requirements of certain life stages. These life stages may include puppy, adult, and obese adult or senior. Other special feeds are designed for active dogs, and those with specific health problems, such as dental disease or diabetes. If your Boxer is younger than 18 months, you will most likely want to go with a quality puppy food. As an adult, your Boxer may not require anything more than a basic, well-balanced adult formula, or it may need a high-performance active dog brand in order to keep its weight down. Senior diets are often packaged to attract purchasers who apply human traits to their dogs and believe that their dogs will be happier eating *more* of *less* food, than less of the food they are currently eating. Some senior foods, however, do have different nutritional values and perhaps digestibility factors that may make them specific to this age group. Again, careful label reading will be able to tell you something about these foods.

What Your Boxer Really Needs

Look for a quality food made by a recognized manufacturer that meets your dog's daily nutritional requirements and is palatable; if it doesn't taste great, it doesn't matter what is in the food—your Boxer won't eat it. The food should show on the label that it has been certified by the American Association of Feed Control Officials (AAFCO) or the Canadian Veterinary Medical Association (CVMA), depending on where you live. The AAFCO and CVMA certifications confirm that the food has been assessed in feeding trials for a certain life stage. In other words, instead of simply providing a nutrient analysis, these certified foods have undergone feeding trials to prove

that they at least meet minimal standards. It would be nice if there were more refined tests that could gauge the exact standards that are met, but at this time there are no requirements for refined testing.

Feeding Holistically

Another option that is available to owners is to prepare fresh meals for your Boxer. Though this method takes time and requires the close recipe supervision of an holistic veterinarian, it can be done. Owners should be advised that developing fresh meals on a daily basis requires dedication. If your idea of a fresh meal for yourself is popping a frozen dinner in the microwave, opening up a bag of prepackaged lettuce, and pouring on a little bottled dressing, then preparing fresh meals for your Boxer is probably not going to be for you.

If you are willing to try this method, however, owners and veterinarians say it can make a night-and-day difference in the overall health of your dog. You are exposing your dog to few if any preservatives or chemicals. The meals contain fresh meat and vegetables, and supplements tailored to your Boxer's needs. This method is not cheap, nor can any shortcuts be taken. There is not much room for creativity, either. The dog's nutritional requirements need to be met, so don't go substituting or swapping ingredients at whim. Follow your veterinarian's recipe and make only those changes he or she has approved or requested.

When to Feed

Young puppies should have their feeding spaced so that they can eat three times a day. Once your Boxer is a year old, it can be fed twice a day. Though some owners choose for convenience to feed their dogs once a day, it is healthier for your dog to eat two smaller portions, one in the morning and one in the evening.

Your Boxer's feeding should also be scheduled so that you are able to avoid feeding the dog one hour before or after strenuous exercise. Your dog should also have access to fresh, cool water at all times to discourage gulping huge quantities of water immediately before or after eating.

How Much to Feed

Are you feeding your Boxer too much, too little, or just enough? While a puppy is growing and maturing, it is particularly important not to overfeed. Though a roly-poly puppy looks cute, this extra weight could possibly begin the destructive cycle of hip dysplasia or cause other mus-

The importance of providing cool, fresh water to your Boxer 24 hours a day cannot be overemphasized.

Controlled feeding is the best choice for most dogs.

culoskeletal problems. Excessively heavy adults and seniors put more strain on their joints as well as their organs. So, be kind; don't overfeed.

It is equally important, especially with puppies, that all of the puppy's nutritional needs are met. If puppies are too thin or are given food that does not provide them with the nutrients they need, the results can be disastrous.

In order to determine if your Boxer is too thin, too fat, or just right, feel the flesh covering your dog's ribs. If you exert slight pressure and can't feel any ribs, your Boxer needs to begin cutting back on its daily intake. (If you're not exercising your Boxer, this can be a factor, too.) If you exert slight pressure and feel the dog's ribs, it is most likely about where it should be on the scale. If you don't even have to push on your dog's sides to feel ribs, you will need to increase your dog's body weight. If a thin dog is eating but not gaining weight, be sure to have your veterinarian rule out that your dog's thinness is not being caused by parasites or disease.

How to Feed

Once you've determined what type of food to feed your dog and when to feed it, you may still have questions as to how to feed it. Some Boxers, if fed dry food, can be allowed to "free feed" without gaining excessive weight. The dog simply takes a nibble here or there from its bowl until by evening the entire helping is finished. Problems that can occur with this feeding method are that if food is left out for long periods of time, it can become stale or infested with bugs; it may attract rats or mice to the dog's dinner bowl; and, of course, there are those Boxers that would eat their entire day's rations in one swift feeding, spending the rest of the day begging for more.

Controlled or rationed feeding is often the better choice for many dogs. In this manner, the dog's total daily allotment of food is divided into two or three servings. The meal is put down only during these scheduled feeding times. To discourage the attraction of insects or other undesirable creatures, many owners pick up whatever food remains after 20 minutes. This is a long enough time to allow your Boxer to leisurely eat its food without making it feel threatened that the bowl is going to be picked up at any time.

Changing Foods— Gradually

Is your dog not doing well on its current food? If so, make the changeover to a new food, gradually. Sudden changes can cause bouts of diarrhea.

To switch over with a minimal amount of agony, use a ten-day plan: During a period of ten days, begin substituting larger amounts of the new food in with the dog's old food. For example, the first day, give your Boxer nine parts of "old" food, one part of new food, the second day, eight parts of "old" food, two parts of new food. Continue mixing each day until finally you are feeding all new food.

Chapter Ten

Preventive Care

Your Boxer's good looks alone will not keep it healthy. Regular exercise, fresh water, good-quality food, and frequent brushing all help to cultivate a sleek, muscular Boxer, but scheduled preventive veterinary care will go far in helping your Boxer to live well into its senior years.

Veterinary Care

One study found that if an owner has provided his or her dog with little or no veterinary care, it is a sign that an owner is giving up on the dog and it will soon be headed for a shelter because the owner doesn't care what is going to happen to it. Obviously, if you are taking the time to read up on the Boxer and learn about its traits and care requirements, you care. And, you're going to make sure your puppy or adult receives the quality veterinary care it deserves throughout its life.

Regular Care

"My Boxer is healthy. Why do I need to pay a veterinarian to tell me that?" Well, for one thing, peace of mind. As a dog owner, hearing that your new puppy is disease-free is great news. Learning that your adopted adult Boxer has no signs of hip dysplasia and will not suffer from this debilitating disease is great news, too.

But the importance of regular veterinary care goes beyond the value of confirming good or bad health suspicions. It is key in preventing a myriad of diseases that can attack and cripple or kill a healthy Boxer. With the vaccines that are available today, and those that will become available in future years, there is no reason for a Boxer to die of any preventable disease.

For diseases that are not preventable—at least not at this point—regular veterinary care can detect these diseases early and provide either cures or promising treatment. Diseases, however, cannot be detected early if the dog is not seen regularly, at least once a year for adult dogs.

Life with a treasured Boxer is never long enough, so it is crucial that you give your devoted partner the best shot at living a lengthy,

The outstanding condition of this male Boxer is no accident: The glossy coat, bright eyes, and muscle tone of this German Sieger are the result of a lifetime of excellent care.

healthy, and pain-free life. Make sure you are mentally and financially committed to providing good, regular veterinary care for your Boxer.

Conventional Versus Holistic

A conventional or allopathic veterinarian is one who has been trained in practices and treatments that are currently being taught in veterinary colleges in the United States. Conventional veterinary medicine includes diagnostic tools such as X rays and magnetic resonance imaging (MRI). It also includes the use of drugs that have been approved by the FDA and proven to consistently be effective in multiple studies, including double-blind studies in which even the person recording results does not know which group is taking the drug being tested and which group is taking placebos.

Holistic veterinary medicine, also called "alternative" or "complementary" medicine, includes a different set of modalities that may or may not have been proven through the tests of Western medicine. Holistic veterinarians may include acupuncture, chiropractic, Chinese medicine, herbal remedies, homeopathy, flower essences, nutritional supplements, and massage in their repertoire, to name a few of the more commonly used modalities.

But here is where the line drawn between the two practices becomes fuzzy and may be the reason that in the future it may be difficult to label a veterinarian either "conventional" or "holistic." Holistic veterinarians are still licensed veterinarians. They were initially trained in conventional medicine and most blend the two practices, using certain holistic treatments to enhance their services. In cases of severe pain or infection where a holistic modality would take too long to begin working, these veterinarians use conventional painkillers and antibiotics.

Traditional veterinarians are also beginning to recognize the benefits of some holistic modalities, such as acupuncture and herbs, and either are learning these methods or making referrals to specialists in these fields. The interest is so great in many areas of holistic medicine that Western medicine studies are now

Boxers don't live forever, but with good preventive care, you can greatly extend the quality of your dog's life.

being performed in many areas of holistic medicine.

What is the best type of veterinarian for you and your Boxer? It really depends. You can't go wrong with a reputable, highly qualified traditional veterinarian. The problem with some holistic practitioners is that there aren't very many, so in some areas of the country it is difficult to find a practitioner. The other problem is in the practitioner's qualifications: Not all have received the accreditation they need to practice a given modality. For example, for a veterinarian to practice chiropractic, he or she should have had hundreds of hours in classes and have received accreditation from a respected professional organization; a weekend seminar will not be enough.

To make sure a veterinarian is qualified and is not merely hanging out the holistic shingle to attract customers, query him or her as to qualifications. If in doubt, call the accreditation facility and confirm what the veterinarian has told you. Though holistic treatments are touted as safe and gentle, with few if any side effects, holistic veterinarians will quickly warn that any modality that is powerful enough to have an effect is powerful enough to also harm a dog if used improperly or at the wrong dosage.

Finding the Right Veterinarian

If you have a veterinarian you really like from a previous or current pet, you're lucky. If you recently moved to a new town or this is your first dog and you need to find a veterinarian, there are several ways to go about locating a good one.

• If you live in the same town as your breeder, ask your breeder who he or she uses. If your breeder is from another town, chances are he or she will know someone in your area who can give you some recommendations. If your breeder is inexperienced and you don't value that individual's opinion, you will need to search a bit harder.

• A call to the local humane society or nonprofit shelter may give you some clues as to whom you could use.

• If you have neighbors with healthy dogs, ask them, too.

• If you're really stumped for names, you can call the American Animal Hospital Association (AAHA) at 1-800-252-2242 for the name of a practitioner in your area.

Once you have a few names, you'll probably want to make an appointment with one. If you don't hit it off with this veterinarian, keep looking. It doesn't matter how many advanced degrees and titles trail off after a veterinarian's name, if you're not comfortable talking to him or her about your Boxer, you will never be able to tap into the veterinarian's knowledge and expertise. You should attempt to find a veterinarian you feel you could ask the dumbest dog question in the world and not be embarrassed or uneasy. The truth of the matter is, when it comes to questions regarding your Boxer's health or behavior, there are no dumb questions!

When you find a qualified veterinarian you and your Boxer are comfortable with, congratulations; you've just taken a big step toward keeping your Boxer healthy. Now you need to make sure you keep an appointment each year in order to keep your Boxer current on its vaccinations.

Common Contagious Infections

With the vaccinations that are available today, there is absolutely no reason to expose a puppy or an adult dog to any common killers. There are several viruses that continue to kill puppies and adults in large numbers and it is strongly advised that your Boxer be brought up to date on its shots and put on an annual vaccination schedule.

Parvovirus

This virus attacks both puppies and unvaccinated adults and can take two forms: gastrointestinal or myocardial. The gastrointestinal form causes vomiting, severe diarrhea, lethargy, and loss of appetite. It is difficult to treat after a puppy or dog has become infected. A previously healthy dog may survive the virus, but a young puppy or weak, aging dog may not. The coronary form of parvovirus attacks the infected puppy's heart muscles, causing breathing difficulties. Puppies with

this form of the virus cannot nurse because they can't catch their breath. This form is even more severe than the gastrointestinal form and currently has no known treatment. Few puppies ever survive the coronary form of this virus, and those that make it past the initial illness frequently die a few months later from chronic congestive heart failure.

Puppies and dogs become infected with parvovirus by ingesting the virus, which is shed in copious amounts in the stools of infected dogs. The virus can live up to six months if conditions are favorable. In some areas of the country, where these conditions are favorable, parvovirus is seen in large numbers. With an effective vaccine, however, there is no reason for your Boxer puppy to ever have to suffer from this deadly virus. Vaccinations are typically given to puppies at 8, 12, 16, and 20 weeks, followed by an annual booster shot beginning at 12 months.

Coronavirus

This virus is not seen as frequently as it once was, and in some areas of the country, it is considered rare. If contracted, however, the coronavirus can kill a puppy or an older adult. Symptoms of the disease include listlessness, weight loss, diarrhea, and vomiting. Infected dogs also can display an insatiable thirst. Interestingly, the virus can appear with parvovirus, making the infected puppy or dog's risks of death significantly higher. Should you vaccinate against this virus? If your veterinarian says

A Boxer that is up-to-date on all its vaccinations throughout its life will never succumb to many common deadly diseases.

the virus is in your area, then yes, you should. Also, if you plan to travel with your Boxer to other areas of the country, you should also have your dog vaccinated against this disease. Vaccinations for puppies are given at 6, 8, and 12 weeks. Some veterinarians boost corona annually, although other veterinarians feel that this is unnecessary.

Distemper

Another viral disease, distemper is reported to be the leading death-causing disease among puppies aged three to eight months. It is highly contagious and affects a puppy or dog's respiratory, gastrointestinal, and nervous systems. Distemper begins innocently enough as what appears to be a cold—watery

eyes and ears. This discharge becomes quite thick and more symptoms begin to appear: fever, lack of appetite, lethargy, diarrhea, and listlessness. From here bad goes to worse. Left untreated, the disease quickly progresses, causing respiratory problems, diarrhea, and pus-filled blisters in the dog's mouth. The only hope to save a puppy stricken with this virus is to recognize the early symptoms and begin treatment immediately; however, treatment is often unsuccessful. The virus progresses quickly to the dog's brain, which usually means death.

Prevention of this rampant and deadly disease is through a series of vaccinations given at 8, 12, and 16 weeks, followed by an annual booster beginning at 12 months.

Rabies

Many dog owners downplay the importance of a rabies shot. They shouldn't. Rabies is on the rise in the mid-Atlantic and some coastal areas. As housing and humans encroach more and more on natural wildlife habitats, people and their dogs are going to come in contact with more rabid animals in certain areas of the country. Rabid foxes, raccoons, and bats make the news when they are discovered, or worse yet, when they bite a person.

If your vaccinated dog is bitten by a rabid wild animal, or if it kills an animal that proves to be rabid, your dog may be protected but you aren't. Rabies kills humans, too. How can you become infected from your own dog? The virus is generally passed when blood or saliva from the rabid animal infects the blood of the victim. If your dog tangles with a rabid animal and you try to clean your dog without taking the precaution of wearing gloves, you could contract the disease through a tiny break in your skin. If the series of rabies shots is not started immediately, there is no cure for the human victim.

Rabies attacks the nervous system, with symptoms usually appearing between two and eight weeks after the bite occurred. The rabid foaming mouth is the result of a paralyzed throat and muzzle. Once symptoms appear, the paralysis spreads rapidly. When the respiratory system is paralyzed, the infected animal (or human) dies.

If your dog is bitten by a wild animal, wash the wound carefully—with gloves!—and ask your veterinarian if your dog needs an additional rabies vaccination. If your Boxer kills a wild animal, you will want to tell animal control authorities where the dead creature is. They will most likely have the animal tested for rabies, particularly if it left the safety of the woods or underbrush and attacked your dog first.

In addition to the death sentence that rabies gives its unvaccinated canine victims, the continual presence of this disease puts everyone on edge. If your Boxer, for whatever reason, bites a person or another animal, and you haven't vaccinated your dog, it may either be detained in your home for a two-week quarantine, or, if it bit someone, it could possibly be euthanized and tested for rabies. Don't risk the chance of your dog contracting this disease. A rabies shot can be given to a puppy at 16 weeks unless the risk of exposure is very high. Following this initial shot, a booster is given one year after the initial puppy vaccine. Depending on local laws, the Boxer is then revaccinated at one- to three-year intervals.

Along with the rabies vaccination is an identification tag and papers recording the vaccination. Do not lose these. Keep your signed certificate from the veterinarian's office in a file, and attach the rabies tag to your dog's collar. If your Boxer is ever out romping around and gets loose, you may be glad it has the rabies tag on. Dog owners quickly recognize a rabies tag and may be less intimidated about approaching your dog if they can spot a current vaccination tag. It's no guarantee, but if your dog does get loose, it could help with the Boxer's safe return.

Bordetella and Kennel Cough

If you will be traveling with your dog, showing it at dog shows, boarding it at a kennel, or taking it to obedience school, your Boxer will need this vaccination. Basically, if you go anywhere with your dog—even in the neighborhood to meet other dogs and people—you should probably get this vaccination. Boarding kennels will require proof of this vaccination before your dog can be boarded, and training schools require the vaccination before a dog can be enrolled in training classes.

Bordetella bronchiseptica bacteria and parainfluenza viruses are the airborne diseases commonly referred to as kennel cough. When infected with *Bordetella,* the dog will be troubled with a persistent and potentially dangerous respiratory disease. It will have a loud honking cough that will wear on both your dog and your nerves. The parainfluenza viruses cause similar pulmonary problems. The effects can be more severe than respiratory discomfort, however. In puppies, the diseases can cause stunted pulmonary development.

This disease can be treated with antibiotics (for *Bordetella*) and cough suppressants, but it is a long, slow

process toward good health. An easier solution is to vaccinate your puppy or dog and prevent the diseases from ever taking hold. The vaccination is commonly applied nasally on a 6- to 12-month schedule. Some veterinarians follow this with an annual booster shot.

Canine Hepatitis

With a series of four shots given at 8, 12, 16, and 52 weeks, you can prevent your dog from contracting canine hepatitis. This disease is not zoonotic (see page 143), so don't worry that you will catch it from an infected dog. It can be very serious in puppies and adult dogs, causing anything from severe renal damage to death. After the initial shot sequence is given, the dog will not need any further vaccinations.

Lyme Disease

This disease is carried by the deer tick, a tiny tick that is thicker in some areas of the country than others but can be transported to many areas by catching a ride on a bird. Cases of ticks infected with Lyme disease have appeared in isolated and odd places in this manner.

Dogs and humans can become infected with Lyme disease. The disease causes arthritis-like pain in joints among a host of other flu-like symptoms. As the disease progresses, additional symptoms appear. The disease is hard to diagnose in humans, and even harder to diagnose in dogs. A dog can't tell you its joints ache a bit and it just doesn't feel well. Unless you recently pulled a tick from your Boxer, you may not even think to suspect this disease.

If you live in an area that has Lyme disease, at the least you will want to take precautions with your Boxer. Always check it thoroughly for ticks when it comes in from the outdoors. If you find a deer tick, bag it in a recloseable bag and have it tested for Lyme disease. If it tests positive, you can begin treatment of your dog.

If you live in an area where Lyme disease is prevalent, you may want to consider having your dog vaccinated against this disease. The vaccine is not perfect, however, and your dog could be vaccinated and still become infected. The vaccine does lower your dog's risks of becoming infected. For up-to-date counseling on the status of Lyme disease in your area and the effectiveness of the vaccine, talk to your veterinarian who should be able to counsel you and help you make the best decision for your Boxer.

Strep Throat

Now here's a strange one. Dogs can have strep throat without being symptomatic or with very few symptoms. The danger here is that your Boxer can infect *you* with the *streptococcus* bacteria! If it seems that members of your family or you keep getting sick with strep throat over a short period of time, don't be surprised if your doctor suggests you have your Boxer tested. Strep throat

Always check your Boxer carefully when you've been outdoors.

Inoculation Schedule

Disease	6 Weeks	8 Weeks	12 Weeks	16 Weeks	20 Weeks	Annual Booster
Coronavirus	X	X	X			
Distemper		X	X	X		X
Parvovirus		X	X	X	X	X
Rabies				X		1–3 years
Bordetella/ Kennel Cough		X	X			X
Canine Hepatitis		X	X	X		1 year
Lyme Disease						X·

Check with your veterinarian for recommended schedule

is not a disease to take lightly in humans or in dogs, so be sure to have it treated immediately in all cases.

Regional Diseases

In addition to the diseases listed above, there are also diseases that can be found in certain areas of the country. Check with your veterinarian to see if there are any additional vaccinations your Boxer might need in your area or in areas to which you frequently travel.

Internal Parasites

There are a whole host of worms that can infect your puppy or adult Boxer. Though some adults are able to coexist with a mild infestation, most are not healthy when worms are present. A serious parasitic infection can kill a young puppy. Be sure to have your puppy and adult's stool checked when you bring your Boxer in for its regularly scheduled appointment. If you notice chronically soft, loose, or even wormy stools, get to the veterinary clinic. Bloody or phlegmy stools indicate a more serious problem and require immediate attention; if it's after hours, go to the emergency veterinary clinic.

Since many of these parasites can and do infect humans, it is critical that your dog is kept free of infestations and that all family members practice good hygiene. It is advisable to wash your hands after picking up after your dog and even after petting or grooming it. Children are particularly susceptible to becoming infected by your dog's parasites because they tend to put their toys and hands in their mouths.

Basically, don't panic if your dog has worms; just make sure you're

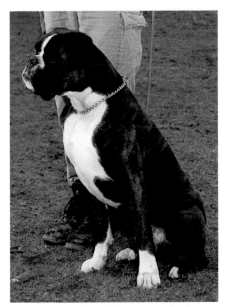
Even well-manicured lawns can harbor unwanted parasites such as worms.

careful and you eradicate the parasites quickly and safely.

Roundworm

This is a very common worm found in puppies. It is acquired by puppies in utero and can also be passed from your puppy or dog to *you*. The eggs are passed in the infected animal's feces; to become infested, the eggs must be ingested. A heavy infestation in puppies can be very damaging. If left untreated, the worms could eventually kill their host. Infected dogs may have a bloated-looking belly, a dull coat, vomiting, and diarrhea.

The good news is that roundworms are treatable, although it may take a series of wormings to rid a dog of the worms. Once the dog is dewormed, you may want to consider giving it a monthly roundworm preventive. Several brands of heartworm preventive medicines include preventives for roundworm as well.

Tapeworm

Fleas, rodents, and rabbits are the intermediate hosts for this worm. If your Boxer loves to go hunting in the woods or is adept at eating fleas, you may run into this worm. Tapeworms are generally not life-threatening in a dog, though they are disgusting. If a dog is infected, it may be relatively free of symptoms, or it may vomit and have diarrhea. It doesn't take a microscope to detect the presence of this worm; bits and pieces of the worm are shed in the dog's stools. Ricelike crawling creatures can also be seen around the anal region.

Fortunately, this worm is fairly easy to eradicate and requires the administration of a wormer. This worm can also infect humans; some species of tapeworm—when in humans—can be fatal. Symptoms can range from mild gastrointestinal discomfort to fatal systemic disease. If you have children, make sure they wash well.

Hookworm

The hookworm is a true bloodsucker. It attaches to the small intestine of the animal where it wines and dines. The blood loss in a puppy from a hookworm infestation can be so severe as to cause death. Bloody stools, diarrhea, and anemia are symptoms. Dogs can become infected either by ingesting eggs, (shed in the feces of an infected animal), or by the hookworm larvae's penetration of the dog's skin. Puppies can become infected through their mother's infected milk.

The worm can be eradicated with medication and prevented with a monthly pill, often combined with a heartworm preventive. Humans can also suffer from a hookworm infection. Commonly, a person will sit on the beach or grass where a dog previously defecated, then the larvae will pierce the person's skin and begin traveling subcutaneously, leaving a red line marking its migration. A human can also accidentally ingest larvae, resulting in gastrointestinal problems. Both infections are treatable but do require immediate medical attention.

Whipworm

If there's a worm that might slip by a diagnosis, it's this one. The eggs of this worm are shed in an infected dog's feces; however, they aren't shed continuously. Once a dog is diagnosed with this worm, the battle is only half over; whipworms are very difficult to get rid of. Part of the problem is that the eggs can live virtually years after they've been shed in the soil, waiting to reinfect another dog. Your own dog can reinfect itself time and time again.

When a whipworm infection is detected, your dog will need to be wormed at least twice over a three-month period, perhaps more. Once your dog is rid of the worms, ask

your veterinarian about the monthly preventive that is available with heartworm medications.

Heartworm

This worm is deadly and can be contracted in nearly every region of the United States. It is very simple to prevent, but costly and sometimes impossible to eradicate without killing the infected host, your dog.

Infected mosquitoes are the culprits in passing this disease to our dogs. The cycle requires that a mosquito with infective larvae injects this into the bloodstream of a dog when the mosquito feeds on the dog. These larvae migrate under the dog's skin to the pulmonary arteries where they lodge and mature into adult heartworms.

Heartworms cause a persistent cough and eventually heart failure. If the dog has a heavy infestation of the worms, exercise may cause it to pass out. The dog may also lose weight, cough up blood, and become very weak. A dog with heartworms may be able to be treated, but much of the success of the treatment depends on the extent

Zoonotic Diseases

No, you don't have to go to the zoo to pick up a zoonotic disease. These are diseases that can be passed from your Boxer *to you.* They include rabies and Lyme disease, as well as several worms: roundworms, tapeworms, hookworms, and giardia.

of the infestation, the age of the dog, and its overall health.

As mentioned above, prevention is easy. Puppies can begin taking heartworm preventive as early as eight weeks and should do so, particularly in high-risk areas of the country. Adult dogs should be tested for the worms, and if free, they can begin taking a regular preventive, too.

Giardia

Think back to your childhood camping days when your counselor cautioned you, "Don't drink stream water without boiling it or treating it."

Make sure your water supply is clean. Well water may harbor dangerous organisms such as giardia.

There was a reason for this: Many streams and rivers contain a microscopic parasite called *giardia,* and if a dog drinks contaminated water, it can become infected. The parasite causes bloating, vomiting, and severe diarrhea. Left untreated, giardia kills both puppies and adults. If a dog is infected with the parasite, it would be wise to separate any other pets from the infected dog until it has finished its course of medication. The parasite can also be passed to a human in a fecal-oral manner.

Be watchful of hygiene while picking up the dog's fecal matter while your pet is infected and during its course of the medication. Children should wash their hands thoroughly after every contact with the dog. You may want to keep them separated as a safeguard, too.

External Parasites

In addition to internal parasites, your Boxer can have external parasites as well. These pests usually are most prevalent in the summer months, but in warm areas of the country, they can be a problem year-round.

Fleas

It's no wonder that these bloodsucking parasites have been around relatively unchanged since prehistoric times. Fleas have survived through the ages because they are resilient, adaptable, and difficult to eradicate. They have been the scourge of mankind and dog- and catdom and have been the carriers of diseases and the cause of many deaths. Besides hurting when they bite, fleas transmit a host of infectious diseases (remember the Black Plague of medieval times?), pass tapeworm infections, and can cause serious allergic reactions. Heavy infestations of fleas can literally drain a small puppy of a substantial quantity of blood.

In addition to causing problems with your dog, fleas can also quickly take over a home. If the fleas have a steady source of food (your Boxer), they will rapidly mature and begin reproducing—laying eggs on your dog, in your rugs, carpets, couches, chairs, and beds. In a short time, a small flea problem can multiply rapidly.

Prevention: Flea prevention is the best solution. There are several products on the market already, with more on the way, that kill adult fleas before they are able to reproduce. If you find a flea on your dog when it's been given this topical treatment, it is a sick flea and it won't last long.

If your dog is already infested with fleas and you fear the worst, that fleas are in your home, most veterinarians will recommend a three-prong approach to ridding your home and dog of the fleas. The key is that the dog and its environment (inside and outside) need to be treated at the same time. If you only rid your dog of its fleas, when the eggs in the carpet hatch the following week, they'll be back. So, treat

your house, the dog's bed, carpeted areas, and anywhere else your dog frequents at the same time you treat your dog. If your yard is infested with fleas, you will need to consider ways to approach this problem as well. Make sure you consult your veterinarian before using any pesticides, however, because these chemicals can be more toxic to your dog than to the fleas you're trying to kill.

You will need to treat your home and dog more than once, too. There is no one product that is capable of wiping out all life stages of the flea at the same time. Therefore, as the eggs hatch, you will need to re-treat your house and dog. Follow your veterinarian's advice carefully and your flea problems should be squashed. Once the fleas are gone, maintain a flea preventive to keep fleas off your Boxer at all times.

Ticks

As discussed earlier in this chapter, ticks can be the carriers of deadly organisms that can affect not only dogs but humans as well. Ticks are hosts to Lyme disease, Rocky Mountain spotted fever, babesiosis and ehrlichiosis. They can also cause a severe reaction in dogs that are sensitive to the tick's saliva, from swelling to paralysis. Tick bites can also be deep and develop into a secondary bacterial infection.

Fortunately, ticks are easy to spot on the Boxer's smooth coat. If you find a tick, remove it immediately with tweezers, grasping the tick as close to the head as possible, and

Depending on your climate, you may have to use preventive measures for fleas and ticks seasonally or year-round.

around the throat area, rush it to the veterinarian; this type of allergic reaction may cut off the dog's breathing.

Prevention: One way to prevent the transmission of disease from ticks is to vaccinate your dog against these organisms. A vaccination for Lyme disease is now available, but it's not perfect. Consult your veterinarian for an up-to-date report. A simpler way is to prevent ticks from biting your dog in the first place. Topical medications and tick-specific collars are available to prevent ticks from biting your dog. Talk to your veterinarian about the possibility of using one of these products during tick season.

Mites

Of the various types of mites—there are several—demodex mites tend to cause the greatest problems among Boxers. The mites live in the dog's hair follicles and sebaceous glands. Demodectic or red mange causes a red, hairless condition. Sometimes Boxer puppies will develop small spots of demodectic mange during teething, possibly linked to the stress of this stage. If the mange cannot be controlled with medications, an improved diet, and perhaps the reduction of the dog's stress, some breeders feel this may be a sign of a more compromised immune system. Mange is not something that you want to see progress, if possible. Work with your veterinarian to help rectify the situation.

pulling straight out without twisting. Leaving the head in can cause an infection. Destroy the tick by crushing it or dropping it into a cup filled with alcohol, gasoline, or turpentine. If you suspect the tick might be a carrier of a disease—if you're in an area where Lyme disease is prevalent—save the tick's body in a reclosable plastic bag and take it to your veterinarian for testing.

Meanwhile, wash your dog's bite area with soap and water and apply an antiseptic. If your dog has never been bitten by a tick before, watch for an allergic reaction. If the dog reacts with hives or begins to swell

Chapter Eleven

Common Diseases of the Boxer

Every breed has particular health problems that seem to crop up more frequently than in other breeds. The Boxer is no different. Though robust in build and strong in mind, the Boxer's health can be crippled by a variety of diseases. With careful breeding, health screenings and tests, and accurate record keeping, it is the hope of conscientious breeders that the occurrence of many of the Boxer's hereditary diseases can be lessened.

Unfortunately, as the Boxer rises in its popularity, the rate of these inherited diseases is expected to climb among those breeders who simply don't care or are unaware of the health of the Boxers they are producing. For this reason, it behooves the future puppy owner to research the breed's common health problems and understand how to test for certain diseases and record the results on a puppy's pedigree. For the owner of an adult Boxer, it is also invaluable to know what types of problems could occur and what kinds of actions can be taken.

Deadly Problems

The top killers of Boxers continue to be various forms of cancer and heart disease. Because these diseases strike young Boxers in relatively great numbers, the life span of a Boxer can be much shorter than the expected ten years. Ongoing research in these areas of disease is helping to determine the inherited characteristics of the diseases in order to prevent them and will someday provide possible cures and treatments. Until further information is known, these diseases will continue to plague Boxers.

In lesser numbers, there are additional diseases and conditions that can prove deadly to Boxers.

Bloat

The precise causes for this disease are not known, but Boxers, as well as other deep- and broad-chested breeds, are susceptible to bloat (gastric dilation-volvulus syndrome or GDV). When a dog suffers from bloat, its stomach becomes

Is your Boxer healthy or does it carry a deadly hereditary disease? Unless you have your dog tested, you may not know until it is too late.

distended with gas and it begins to twist. The gas in the stomach is not produced by the stomach itself; rather, it is "swallowed air" caused by the dog gulping food or water, or following extreme stress or vigorous exercise. As the stomach twists, the flow of gas, fluids, and food from the stomach to the intestines is blocked. The blood supply to the stomach is also cut off. If a dog can be seen by a veterinarian immediately at the onset of this syndrome, it may have a chance for survival. However, if the twisting and strangling of the stomach and intestines are not halted immediately, the Boxer will die in a few hours.

Studies are underway to determine what causes the stomach to begin twisting and why certain breeds are more susceptible than others. Until a definitive answer is determined, Boxer owners are advised to take some precautions to lower the susceptibility of their dogs.
• Feed two or more small meals a day rather than one huge meal.
• Place rubber chew toys in the dog's food to keep it from gulping its meal too fast.

• Allow constant access to cool, fresh water to avoid gulping large quantities.

• Do not feed a Boxer that has recently exercised or is going to exercise. Allow one hour for the dog to cool down after exercising before feeding. If the dog is going to exercise after eating, feed only a small portion of the meal at least one hour before the exercise. The balance of the meal can be fed an hour after the exercise is completed.

• Keep abreast of the latest developments in prevention and treatment of this disease. As research is completed, the techniques recommended to avoid bloat may change. Your veterinarian will be a good source for this information.

Symptoms of bloat: If your Boxer bloats, you have virtually minutes to get help. Knowing what the symptoms of the syndrome are may mean the difference between saving your Boxer or not.

• Uneasiness, restlessness, inability to lie down comfortably

• Repeated nonproductive attempts to vomit

• Drooling

• Breathing rapidly but not deeply

• Gums that are either very pale, very red, or blue

• A bloated or distended appearance to the stomach area

Cancer

Unfortunately, there have been no formal studies to determine which types of cancer strike Boxers with the greatest frequency. Cancer is,

however, one of the leading causes of death among Boxers and can strike both young dogs as well as geriatrics. Cancer is so prevalent that Boxers are considered to be one of the top five breeds most prone to this disease.

Treatments for various types of cancer are costly and have limited success rates, depending on the type of cancer. Some cancers are thought to be inherited; others may

Boxers are susceptible to all sorts of cancers, so if you discover a small bump on any part of your Boxer's body, have your veterinarian examine it immediately.

149

have an environmental origin. Because of the hereditary factor it is important to know how common the incidence of cancer is in various lines when considering purchasing a puppy. A pedigree with very few cases of cancer is not a guarantee by any means that your puppy will not develop the disease, but it is a good hedge.

Degenerative Neuropathy

Older Boxers—those over the age of seven—sometimes display a degenerative disease of the spine. Veterinary neurologists say that in the Boxer this condition is commonly mistaken for spondylosis deformans, which is a bridging of the spinal vertebrae. Spinal disease, regardless of the source, can be quite painful and debilitating. There are currently limited treatments for these diseases, and the onset of degenerative neuropathy often marks the beginning of the decline of the dog.

Heart Diseases

There are two forms of heart disease that plague the Boxer: cardiomyopathy and subvalvular aortic stenosis. Both are hereditary diseases that, with testing, careful record keeping, and wise breeding practices could be lessened substantially in frequency.

Aortic stenosis: This heart disease involves a blockage at or below the aortic valve. If the narrowing of the aorta is severe enough, the blood flow from the heart is restricted. To compensate, the heart's left side works harder to push the blood through the narrow vessel. This increased work makes the laboring side of the heart become overworked and enlarged.

The effects of an aortic obstruction can be noticeable when the affected Boxer is quite young. Weakness and fainting are symptoms of the disease, but puppies have been known to literally "drop dead." Detection of the disease can be made with a thorough veterinary exam, including auscultation of the heart, and a diagnosis confirmed through the use of an ultrasound. Unfortunately, there is not much that can be done to help Boxers suffering from this disease. Surgery is not commonly performed or recommended because the effects are only temporary.

Boxers suffering from AS should not be bred because the disease is thought to be transmitted as an autosomal dominant gene. (If the Boxer *has* the gene for the disease it will have the disease and will pass the disease to its puppies. A recessive gene, in contrast, requires *both* parents to be carriers for *some* of the puppies to inherit the disease.) Littermates of an affected puppy should be tested for AS and only bred if the test is negative because these puppies may also be carrying the gene. The parents should be examined too, to determine which dog—or if both—are carrying the gene for this disease.

Cardiomyopathy: The hallmark of this heart disease is an arrhythmia

Boxer cardiomyopathy is not a disease of the elderly; it can strike Boxers of any age and should be tested for at a young age.

or abnormal heart rhythm. Many dogs do not show any signs of the disease until they die suddenly and unexpectedly. Other dogs may show symptoms such as fainting or weakness after exercise. In some cases, the dog's heart may become enlarged or dilated, but experts say this is uncommon and may actually be a separate form of the disease.

Recent studies suggest that this disease is inherited in an autosomal dominant manner. The difficulty in breeding out this heart disease is that the clinical symptoms of the disease sometimes do not appear until the Boxer is older and most likely has already been bred, perhaps repeatedly.

Diagnosis can be difficult. Unlike the form of cardiomyopathy that plagues other breeds, the Boxer's heart is not enlarged. An electrocardiogram (ECG) can be used to detect premature ventricular contractions, which are thought to be early warning signs of developing cardiomyopathy. However, the standard ECG strip of five minutes or less is ineffective in picking up the intermittent arrhythmia that is seen in many Boxers. The Holter Monitor is the diagnostic test of choice for Boxers because it records a 24-hour ECG. Subtle arrhythmias can often be detected in this longer test. Boxers have been diagnosed as young as six months by using this method of testing.

It is strongly advised to begin routinely examining young and middle-aged Boxers for signs of developing this disease. Unfortunately, a positive diagnosis for the disease helps the breeder eliminate this disease from his or her lines, but it does not help the affected dog. There is no known cure for this disease. Treatments range in their effectiveness and may include the use of the nutritional supplements such as L-carnitine or medical therapy to strengthen the heart and to control abnormal rhythms.

Heatstroke: Brachycephalic or short-nosed breeds may be able to breathe better than a long-nosed dog when holding an attacker's arm; however, the selective breeding that produced this bite and short muzzle also produced a breed that does not tolerate heat well at all. Dogs cool themselves by panting. Longer-nosed dogs are able to cool themselves much more efficiently than short-nosed breeds.

Adding to the problem of not being able to cool themselves efficiently, Boxers don't seem to realize this. Most will be quite eager to run, jump, play, and cavort about in the most severe heat. Carrying a favorite toy or retrieving balls compounds the problem, because the Boxer is even more limited when it comes to cooling itself. Veterinary experts say that by the time your Boxer begins to show signs of overheating, you already have a serious problem on your hands.

Signs of heatstroke include rapid panting, weakness, tiredness, an elevated temperature (above 105°F [40.6°C]), dark red to purple gums and tongue, even disorientation. The dog may also be dehydrated, which can be determined by lifting its skin above its shoulders and observing how quickly it returns to its normal shape. Have your veterinarian show you in advance what "healthy" skin looks like.

If the Boxer has become overheated, move it quickly to a shady spot and soak with cool, not cold, water. Transport the dog to the veterinarian as quickly as possible. Heatstroke can be prevented by minimizing your Boxer's activities in high temperatures and keeping a close eye on it in warmer weather. A Boxer should never be left outdoors for any period of time, especially during the summer. Cool, fresh water should be available at all times, as well as a shady, comfortable spot.

Histiocytic ulcerative colitis: Boxers are susceptible to this disease with such frequency that some experts refer to it as "Boxer ulcerative colitis." The disease is believed to be genetic and is best avoided by studying breed lines that have tracked the disease's occurrence.

In general, colitis is an inflammation of the colon. With Boxers, there is a tendency to develop deep ulcers in the colon wall, making the disease particularly painful. Defecation is abnormal with this disease, often diarrhetic. The stools may contain mucus and some blood.

Because the Boxer tends to develop deep ulcerations, the colitis becomes more than an inconvenient irritation. Treatments to help control the disease and offer some comfort to the dog include strict diets of bland foods and antibiotics. There is no known cure for the disease, which can progress until it reaches the point of becoming painfully relentless. Diagnosis is made from intestinal biopsies.

Nonlife-threatening Diseases

The following diseases are not life-threatening to the Boxer, but they do appear in Boxers with some regularity. For this reason, Boxer owners should be aware of them and be knowledgeable in the symptoms of the diseases so that prompt, expert veterinary treatment can be provided.

Acne

In many breeds of dogs, acne is a puppy problem. With Boxers, this unsightly problem can extend into adulthood. As with humans, acne in Boxers is caused by clogging in the dog's hair follicles or pores. The acne appears on the dog's chin, often around the time the puppy begins to develop hormonally or during its teen months (8 to 18 months). Treatment for dog acne is much the same as with humans. Acne cleansing pads are sometimes prescribed to clear the dog's pores. Warm soaks can help to pull the infection from the pores. In more severe cases, a veterinarian may prescribe topical scrubs, gels, or creams.

Spinal disorders can make life difficult for aging Boxers; however, depending on the afflicted Boxer, some mechanical assistance can help extend the dog's quality of living.

Corneal Ulcers

Another disease that appears to be genetic, the appearance of ulcers on the surface of a Boxer's eyes may appear in older Boxers. Because the disease does not appear until the dog is older, it is a difficult one to breed out.

Symptoms of a corneal ulcer include excessive watering in the eye or signs of pain. Though not considered life-threatening, corneal ulcers do affect the vision of the dog and can become very uncomfortable.

Currently, there are no treatments that are 100 percent effective in correcting the situation; however, some Boxers have responded well to surgery in which the damaged cornea is trimmed away. Collagen is sometimes applied to the cornea, or the use of therapeutic contact lenses may be prescribed.

Cushing's Syndrome

Also referred to as hyperadrenocorticism, Cushing's syndrome is a disease in which the pituitary gland causes an excess of cortisol to be produced in the body. In some cases, a malfunction of the adrenal glands may also cause the rise in cortisol. Tumors on either gland are often the culprit.

Symptoms of the disease vary but often include symptoms similar to diabetes: excessive thirst, appetite, increased urination. Boxers suffering from the disease may also appear lethargic or suffer hair loss. Diagnosis for the disease can be made through a variety of available screening tests.

Treatment for Cushing's syndrome depends on the source of the disease. Pituitary disease is often treated with medications; adrenal disease may require surgery.

Ear Infections

Whether your Boxer's ears are cropped or natural, chances are it may suffer an ear infection sometime in its life. Researchers say ear infections are most commonly caused by allergies, followed by foreign bodies in the ear. Both conditions can cause an imbalance in the bacteria and yeast naturally found in the dog's ear. Cropped ears do not provide a hedge against getting an infection; in fact, the upright ears may enable foreign bodies such as burrs and other vegetation to lodge themselves deeply in the ear. Veterinary experts emphasize that the pendulous "natural" ears *do not* cause infections; however, the warmer, moister environment of the natural ear may increase the rate that the infection, which started for *other* reasons, grows.

Ear infections generally can be detected early by regularly smelling the dog's ears. An infection will be foul smelling and strong. The owner may also notice excessive discharge coming from the ear. When an ear infection is detected, it should not be ignored. Untreated infections can lead to middle and inner ear infections, which are much more serious and much more difficult to treat.

Elbow Dysplasia

Many different diseases can affect the elbow joint of a Boxer and cause permanent and progressive damage. Often, the first warning an owner has that his or her Boxer has elbow dysplasia is when the dog suddenly can't walk or put weight on its front legs. The elbow joints are hot with inflammation, and arthritis begins its destruction in the joint.

Diagnosis of the disease involves X-raying the dog's elbow joints and sending the X-rays to either the Orthopedic Foundation for Animals (OFA) or the Genetic Disease Control in Animals (GDC). Registry numbers are assigned by both organizations to Boxers that are free of disease. In dogs with elbow dysplasia, OFA grades the degree of dysplasia from I (a slight case) to III (full-blown degenerative joint disease). Since elbow dysplasia is thought to be a genetic disease, Boxers with *any* degree of the disease should not be bred. Though there is no cure for elbow dysplasia, preventive measures—or those things that may help prevent the onset of the disease in a dog that is predisposed to the disease—may include the following: maintaining a healthy body weight (not fat), avoiding excess calcium and protein in developing dogs, and providing easy, regular exercise for young dogs.

Hip Dysplasia

This crippling disease is thought to be genetic. Interestingly, and frustratingly to some breeders, some dogs with hip dysplasia can live their lives without ever showing clinical signs of the disease. The disease for these dogs only appears on an X ray. Current theory holds that these dogs are predisposed to the disease, but may not have developed symptoms of hip dysplasia because of certain environmental factors.

At any rate, this disease is degenerative, which means that once the cycle of destruction begins in the joint, it is very hard to slow, perhaps unlikely that it can be completely halted, and impossible to reverse. As mentioned above, diagnosis for the disease is by X ray, which is taken between one year and two years of age, depending on the type of X ray taken and the registering body. Registration of clear hips is maintained by OFA, GDC, and PennHIP.

Once a dog is determined to be dysplastic, treatment varies with the symptoms of the dog, the dog's age, and the progression and destruction of the disease. Many treatments are showing promise, including some holistic modalities, in slowing the progression of this disease. In severely crippled dogs, surgery may be the only option.

Preventive measures include selecting a puppy from a breeder who has registered at least three generations of Boxer hips as free of disease, but this, of course, is not a guarantee of clear hips in the puppy, yet; in the future, it may be. For now, however, puppy owners need to take preventive measures in feeding their Boxer puppies food that meets but does not exceed their nutritional requirements. Nutritional supplements such as calcium, phosphorous, and vitamin D have been

A Boxer suffering from hip dysplasia may become severely limited in its activities—unlike this healthy fawn.

shown in studies to exacerbate growth problems. Also, exercise should not be extreme, but rather should be easy and steady, such as jogging and swimming, so that the hip joints do not suffer any trauma. The buildup of muscles around the joint is also believed to be beneficial to the hips in preventing dysplasia.

Hypothyroidism

Any time a Boxer becomes lethargic, its owner should start looking for answers. One reason may be that the Boxer is suffering from hypothyroidism in which thyroid hormones are produced in insufficient quantities. Hair loss is seen in some Boxers suffering from hypothyroidism, but more than half never show this symptom. Some Boxers may simply be suffering recurrent infections.

The disease is difficult to diagnose, but with the battery of tests now available, if a veterinarian suspects this disease, diagnosis is possible. Treatment is lifelong but is relatively easy—a hormone supplement taken once or twice daily. The only difficulty is that the diagnosis must be accurate and can't be an educated guess because excess thyroid hormones can affect the heart.

Uterine Inertia

Some Boxer bitches require cesarean sections because the uterus fails to contract or the contractions are so weak the puppies cannot be delivered. This condition may prevent labor from ever starting or it may develop during labor and shut down deliveries. The situation is an emergency and no time should be wasted taking the laboring female to the veterinarian.

Vaginal Hyperplasia

If your Boxer bitch is spayed, she will never suffer from this disease. Vaginal hyperplasia is seen in Boxers and is caused by an abnormal response to estrogen. (Removing the dog's ovaries, part of the spaying process, eliminates the surges of estrogen production.) When a female begins a heat cycle, the surge in estrogen causes a mass of tissues to bulge out of the vaginal opening. The tissues can be damaged by the female's licking, chewing, or sitting on the mass. The obstructing mass may prevent attempts to breed the Boxer. When the heat cycle is over, the mass generally disappears.

Chapter Twelve
The Well-behaved Boxer

There are many reasons why you should not only make sure your Boxer is trained, but trained well.

1. A Boxer that will sit, stay, lie down, and come when called is a manageable dog. If the dog is consistent in its responses to commands, it becomes a reliable dog. A reliable, manageable Boxer can be taken virtually anywhere with its owner and will be completely controllable. Imagine the places you can take your Boxer knowing that you won't be dragged across the street or have your dog attempt to have a confrontation with every dog that comes within a half-mile radius. You'll also be confident that your Boxer will respond in a friendly manner to everyone you meet *because you've trained it to respond this way.*

2. Your training efforts will help to establish you in the leadership role. When your family is also involved in the Boxer's training, the entire family shifts into this leadership role, too. When the "boss" or "bosses" are accepted by your dog, you generally will have little if any problems with your Boxer attempting to dominate you or your children. And if you *do* have problems, because you are training your dog, your trainer will be able to give you expert advice to help you work through these problems.

3. The time you spend with your dog will strengthen the human-animal bond. Yes, your Boxer will love you just because you're you, but it will love you even more—and you will appreciate your Boxer more—if you become active partners. Obedience training is an excellent way to begin this process.

4. The exercise, both mental and physical, that your Boxer will get from being trained is stimulating. The Boxer is a working dog and loves to have a job to do. If there's no job, your Boxer will likely assign itself one to keep from becoming too bored. The only problem with this self-appointed job is it probably is something you'd rather your Boxer *not* do, such as rearrange the furniture or relandscape your backyard. So, give your dog a job and watch it flourish!

5. If you train your Boxer to be a gentleman or lady, you will be more popular. Neighbors will invite you to cookouts, your boss will give you a raise, and—well maybe training your Boxer won't produce such dramatic results in your social life, but whether your neighbors say it or not, they will appreciate living next to people who care for their dog and who they feel are responsible owners. You may never hear a compliment verbally, but had you not trained your Boxer and had you left it to its wild ways, *you would have heard a lot,* and none of it would have been good.

Finding a Good Training Center

You plan on training your puppy or adopted adult Boxer, but where do you go? The good news is that there are trainers everywhere that are eager to get you started. The bad news is that all trainers do not have equal skills; in fact, the skills of some trainers are questionable at best. To make sure you find a trainer who will meet your needs, you'll need to do a little research.

1. The first place to begin is to ask professionals you trust in related fields for referrals. Your veterinarian should be an excellent source. If you purchased your puppy from a reputable breeder in your area, he or she will also know whom to go to and whom to avoid. If you adopted a Rescue Boxer, your contact with the rescue will have referrals in the area.

What Is Puppy Preschool?

Early training for puppies aged ten weeks and older is commonly referred to as puppy preschool or puppy kindergarten. In these classes, young puppies learn the basics *and* continue their important lessons in socialization during puppy "playtime." If there is one class that should not be missed, the early puppy class is it. It's fun for the whole family and begins shaping the puppy's lifetime behaviors.

2. Once you have a short list of trainers and/or training centers to check out, make some phone calls. Find out when classes are scheduled and ask if you can visit a class prior to enrolling. If you are not allowed to visit, then discontinue the conversation. Training techniques are never so secret that you can't watch. More likely, the trainer is using techniques that aren't necessarily productive or positive. If you're allowed to visit a class, do it.

3. When you are in the class, watch the owners' responses to the trainer as well as the dogs' reactions. If the owners are hesitant or quiet, they may be used to being barked at a bit—by the trainer. If the dogs are seen giving the trainer the wary eye, there's a good reason for it, and you don't have to stay to figure it out. Go. Find another trainer.

What you are looking for is an enthusiastic, knowledgeable trainer both the owners and the dogs enjoy.

A manageable Boxer can be taken almost anywhere with confidence and control.

at least two series of vaccinations, a rabies vaccine and a current kennel cough vaccine. This requirement is to protect your puppy from catching a life-threatening disease from an infected dog, and to protect other dogs from potentially catching something from an unvaccinated puppy. Adult dogs will be required to have the same minimums or may be required to have completed their series of vaccinations.

Body Language

Dogs are very visual and they are attracted to certain body styles. A world-class Schutzhund trainer once said that "the body talks." He felt that the best trainers were those who were able to communicate with their dogs through their bodies—the way they walked, the way they carried themselves, the way they reacted to their dogs' performances. Handlers who were stiff and restrained with their dogs were less effective in communicating and were less productive with their training.

For owners of companion dogs, the lesson to be learned is to express yourself. Don't worry what anyone might think, focus on your dog's reactions. You might be surprised at what you see.

You also want the training methods to be strictly through positive reinforcement. Harsh corrections should never be used with young puppies and are rarely warranted with adult dogs. When observing the class, you should see lots of wagging tails, tons of praise, and an upbeat trainer.

4. Once you have found a good trainer or center, sign up for classes. Good schools fill their classes quickly. If you are purchasing a puppy, make sure you are aware of the vaccination requirements of the school and the minimum age requirements. Many schools require

Teaching the Basics

If there is not a school in your area or if you couldn't get a place reserved in a class for a couple of months, you can begin training the basics to your Boxer at home. There are many good books on the market for beginning puppy training and basic obedience for older dogs; however, some of the best sources are videos or video/book combinations (see Useful Addresses and Literature, page 198). Videos give the beginner a visual grasp of concepts that are sometimes hard to grasp when reading a written description.

Using Treats

The use of treats to condition a dog to respond to a command in a certain way has been criticized by some trainers. Their reasoning is that if you use treats, the dog will work only for treats. Don't listen to them.

Initially, yes, your Boxer will live to work for treats. As a bottomless pit, it would do anything to get a yummy morsel. Use this to your advantage. Reward every time the dog performs the requested behavior until the dog's response is consistent. Once you've achieved consistency, you can begin to cut out the treats, alternating praise rewards alone with praise rewards and treats. Your Boxer will continue to perform, anticipating that it will get a treat at some point.

To get you started, the following are the basic commands you will want to begin teaching your puppy or adult. Remember, keep the lessons positive. The trick is to reward and praise your Boxer when you catch it doing something right.

Watch Me

One of the hardest things to achieve with a puppy is to get it to pay attention to you for more than a nanosecond. Sometimes it seems that it's hard just to get the puppy to recognize that you've said its name (maybe it doesn't know its name!). To get your Boxer to begin recognizing that it needs to watch you when you say its name, begin playing the *watch me* game. This works for adult Boxers who are new to training, too.

Take a nice fragrant treat, such as hot dogs cut into little pieces or dog

A treat is passed over the Boxer's head.

161

jerky, and, holding it in your fingertips, put it close enough under your Boxer's nose to get its attention. Bring the morsel up under your chin and say, *"Watch me,"* or the dog's name, *"Ginny!"* When the dog looks at you, immediately reward it with the treat. As the puppy or dog gets the hang of the game, you can hold the treat under your chin and move around a bit. Feel free to act silly; your Boxer will love the show. Reward the Boxer for watching you. You will notice that your Boxer will quickly focus on you whenever you give it the *watch me* command or say its name.

The Boxer naturally sits to track the treat.

If you're home during the day, perform this exercise intermittently throughout the day; you will want to walk around with a hip pack filled with prechopped treats. If you work away from the home, try this exercise in the morning, after you get home, and intermittently until you retire for the night. Keep it fun and praise, praise, praise when your Boxer does it right.

Sit

This command may be the most helpful behavior you ever teach your Boxer. A dog that bolts out that door can be put on a *sit.* A growing puppy that wants to jump up and grab the food bowl out of your hands can be put on a *sit* until the food is set on the floor. A *sit* prevents a boisterous Boxer from jumping up on unsuspecting visitors. The *sit* is also a simple exercise to teach your dog.

The old manner of teaching the *sit* involved holding the dog's collar and gently pushing the dog's rump to the floor while saying, *"Sit."* This may work with very young puppies, but there are very few, if any, individuals who will have the strength to wrestle an adult Boxer's haunches to the ground if the Boxer would prefer to stand. So, clever trainers developed a more positive, reward-based method of teaching the *sit* that allows a hand signal to be taught at the same time.

Put a treat in your hand and wrap your fingers around it. While holding your Boxer gently by the collar, pass the hand with the treat slowly from the dog's nose—to give it a scent—to the top of its skull. As the dog shifts its weight to track the treat, it naturally sits. After you've rewarded it for sitting with praise and the treat, release it with an exuberant release command, such as *"OK!"*

With a little practice, your Boxer soon will be eagerly sitting every time you say *"Sit."* In the early stages, *always* reward with a treat, and with lots of enthusiastic praise. Also, make sure you give the command only when you are in a position to enforce it. In other words,

don't teach your Boxer that it may not have to sit if you give the command out of arm's reach. Keep your training consistent and positive.

Sit-Stay

This is the *sit* command with an added bonus—a *stay.* Once your dog is sitting consistently with the *sit* command, you can begin adding the *stay.* Attach a leash to your dog's collar and put it in a *sit.* Now, holding the leash slightly taut—just enough to "feel" where the Boxer is—give your dog the *"Stay"* command (verbally) along with the *stay*

Keep some tension in the leash as you begin your walk around the dog during the sit-stay.

Repeat the stay *command as needed.*

command (visually). The visual command for the *"stay"* is either a right-to-left short sweep of the hand in front of the dog's nose, or simply the hand in front of the nose. Once you have verbally told your dog to stay, begin walking around the dog counterclockwise, keeping the leash barely taut, repeating the verbal command *"Stay"* as needed to steady your dog. If your Boxer begins to stand, repeat the *sit* command, return to the dog's right side, and begin the *stay* exercise again.

When your Boxer successfully completes the *sit-stay* exercise,

release it with an *"OK"* and reward and praise it.

Down

The *down* command is a natural progression from the *sit,* so you'll want to make sure your puppy or adult understands the concept of sitting on command. The *down* command is particularly good to use when you are going to be somewhere with your Boxer and you want it to be comfortable, but you also want it to be in control. The *down* position is a more submissive position for a dog and can be used to

With the dog in a sit, *pass the treat from under the dog's nose out and down to the ground.*

As the dog tracks the treat, it will lie down.

help reinforce the handler's leadership. Dogs are also less likely to bark in the *down* position, so this command also has its usefulness with barking Boxers.

To teach the *down,* put your Boxer in a *sit.* Then, while gently holding the dog's collar, take the treat and slowly move it from the dog's nose down to the ground. If your Boxer is steady in its *sit,* it will naturally move to a *down.* If it is less steady in its *sit,* it may try to pop up its haunches and rock forward to retrieve the treat. If this happens, put your Boxer back in a *sit* and repeat the exercise. Eventually, the *down* will become a regular part of your dog's repertoire, too.

Down-Stay

The *down-stay* is taught in the same manner as described for the *sit-stay* except the Boxer begins the *stay* in the *down* position. As your dog becomes more reliable on its *stays,* begin moving a little distance away from it, always keeping it on a leash. Using a recall leash—30 feet (9 m)—begin varying the distances you move from your dog during the *down* and *sit-stays.* Again, never take your dog off the training leash; never give it a chance to fail. Once your dog can be trusted at a distance, increase the time at which you stay at the end of the long leash.

Stand-Stay

The *stand-stay,* which is very convenient for veterinary exams and grooming, is taught in the same way as the *sit-stay* and *down-stay,* except the dog is, of course, standing. With your Boxer standing on your left side, first give the command *"Stand,"* and then the command *"Stay."* While holding the leash taut, slowly walk around your dog, repeating the command *"Stay"* as necessary. Once your dog stands still as you walk around it, you can practice the exercise standing further away from the dog—while on leash.

Come

The recall command, when heeded, saves lives. No matter how careful an owner is, there is always that one instance in which your Boxer slips away and heads straight for the road. If you've taught your Boxer the recall command, your chances of it turning and coming back or perhaps just stopping are far greater than if you have not trained your Boxer at all.

With puppies and with adults, the recall command can begin as a game. If you have several family members, or friends who enjoy your Boxer, have them sit in a large circle in a fenced yard. One at a time, take turns calling the Boxer to you. Anything goes. Get down on the ground. Clap your hands. Act silly, but do whatever it takes. When the Boxer comes, give it lots of love, praise it wildly. Then have another member in the circle do the same thing. Pretty soon, the Boxer will associate coming as something good.

When your Boxer has mastered the *sit-stay,* you can perform this

Begin the recall as an on-leash exercise at a short distance.

For now, you want that enthusiasm and you want a speedy and reliable recall. It may just save your Boxer's life someday.

Note: Selective hearing is a frustrating trait of the Boxer; stubbornness is another. Without a doubt, Boxers can be a challenge to train. They can also take their sweet time coming when you call them. In real-life situations, your Boxer will not have a leash on when you desperately want it to come; that's *why* you want it to come. Regardless of how long it takes for your dog to return to you and no matter how much calling and clapping and silliness you have to do to regain your dog's attention, *never* punish your dog for coming. Always praise it. Your Boxer will remember the last action you take. If you scold it for coming, what are your hopes of ever having it come again? If you praise it, your Boxer may even come back a little faster next time.

exercise solo. Put the Boxer on a *sit-stay,* walk out to perhaps 5 feet (1.5 m) on the recall leash, and call your dog. Praise it enthusiastically for coming. Keep working at greater distances until your Boxer literally can gain enough speed to bowl you over. If it does, don't worry; you can think about adding another *sit* command on the end of the recall later.

Praise your dog enthusiastically when it comes to you.

You can then add a sit *command at the end of the recall.*

Walk Nicely

If there's one thing that Boxers *aren't* known for, it's nice walking manners. Invariably, you'll see a 65-pound (29-kg) hulking male Boxer dragging its owner around the block, going wherever it pleases. Why? Because when the Boxer is a puppy it naturally follows its owners around. It's also easy to exercise a puppy in a small area, such as a backyard, so a leash isn't needed. But walking puppies on leashes is *very* important if you want to have control later.

As soon as you get your puppy home, you can begin working on the *walk nicely* exercise. Basically, the exercise requires that you use your voice to keep the Boxer puppy close to you. If the puppy strains on the leash, stop and use your voice to bring the puppy back into you. No pops or jerks are necessary in this exercise. Just lots of attention and a few treats. Change directions quickly and encourage the puppy to stay with you too. Work on this exercise several times a day, every day, and your Boxer will catch on quickly. Gradually, you can work this exercise into heeling, in which the Boxer must stay at your side, looking up at you attentively as it trots.

Use your voice to keep your dog close to your side. If your dog surges ahead, make sharp turns to keep the dog's attention on you and where you are walking.

The Art of House-training

A good training chapter wouldn't be complete without a section on the most rudimentary of training basics: house-training. Fortunately for Boxer owners, the breed tends to be very fastidious when it comes to hygiene. Boxers don't like to lie in or near their urine or waste, which works to the owner's advantage. The key is to set your puppy or adult up for success and minimize its chances for failure.

When a Dog Needs to "Go"

In addition to first thing in the morning and last thing at night, there are several times your Boxer will need to relieve itself during the day: after exuberant play, after eating, immediately upon exiting the crate, and, if it's a puppy, every two hours while it's awake. You're now thinking, "Is there any time this dog *doesn't* have to "go?" If you want to house-train your Boxer quickly with few to no mistakes, the answer is, "In the beginning it's better to be safe than to be investing money in steam cleaners and spot removers."

Crate Training

The use of a crate is one of the fastest ways to train your dog that outside is where the "potty" is and inside is strictly off limits. As mentioned earlier, the Boxer doesn't like to be dirty. If the dog is left in a room by itself, it can happily run behind the couch and relieve itself there, but if the Boxer is in a crate, it has nowhere to go, so it won't unless it really has to.

Your job is to predict when your Boxer will need to go and to walk it or take it outside. Follow your Boxer and when it finds a spot, praise it gently *while it is in the act of relieving itself.* You may feel a little silly following your dog around the yard, but the praise works. Remember, catch it in the act of something good and reward it. You can even give the dog a treat right after it has relieved itself in the correct place.

House-training takes consistency (always allow the dog to relieve itself regularly) and positive reinforcement (praise and treats). Also, never give your Boxer too much freedom too soon. Take baby steps. The Boxer must associate that (1) the crate is home and it mustn't dirty the crate, (2) the room in which the crate is housed is home and this area mustn't be soiled either, and (3) all the rooms in this wonderful home are "inside" and they are all off limits! This association is very gradual for puppies. Adult dogs may make the association much faster, but still don't allow them to fail.

Mistakes Will Happen

You just walked your Boxer, it relieved itself, and you brought it inside to enjoy a few minutes with you in the newly carpeted family room. A few seconds later, you discover that your Boxer left you a present. Take two steps back in the house-training game. What do you do?

If you discover the mistake after the fact, do nothing. Do *not* yell at your Boxer and definitely do *not* physically correct it. Your Boxer thinks in the present and will associate any verbal or physical correction with its current behavior: "Hey, I was lying nicely in my bed and you just came in and scolded me." Shame on you. Instead, get your cleanup supplies and take care of the mess. If you have a puppy, put the puppy in its crate, with no malice, so that it will not attempt to play with you while you're scrubbing the floor.

The time to correct your puppy is when it is *in the act.* If you catch your puppy as it is relieving itself, grab the puppy and say, *"No!"* firmly. Rush the puppy out to the yard, place it in a suitable spot and praise it gently when it does the right thing. Give it a treat, clean up the mess inside, and forget about it. Do remember, however, to keep a closer eye on your dog the next time.

Potty Commands

Yes, you can teach your Boxer to relieve itself on command. Every time you take your dog outside specifically to relieve itself, say *"Go potty,"* or some other related code that only you and your Boxer will know. Repeat this command several times every time your puppy or dog relieves itself. Soon, you will be able to take your dog out and give it the *potty* command, and your Boxer will start looking for a spot.

Why would you want to teach your dog this type of command? If you travel with your dog, you will immediately know why. Rest stops can be few and far between. When you find one, you can't be picky. If your dog is used to relieving itself only on mulched beds or on closely cropped grass, it may be uncomfortable in other locations. Still, if you've trained it to relieve itself on command, it will try to go anywhere. *Go potty,* is an extremely helpful command and a real time-saver, too.

Other House-training Tools

Dog doors: Dog doors can be a tremendous convenience. The flexible door is set into a storm door, allowing the dog to go in and out at will. This door can be a great way to facilitate house-training with young dogs because it allows the Boxer to relieve itself when it needs to, not just when you're around. The door must open into a fenced backyard on one side, and into a protected area of the house on the other. Ideal locations for dog doors are in washrooms that exit into the yard on one side. If gated into the washroom, there's not much for the Boxer to destroy. A hard, scrubbable floor is also a prerequisite for the room inside the dog door.

Pitfalls of dog doors are that the Boxer must learn to use it and not abuse it, considering it a fun chew toy. Also, though the door gives your dog more freedom during times when you're not home, it also allows your dog more freedom to drag things into your home, including mud, mulch, and plants it didn't like in the flower bed. Some folks worry that a dog door will allow strange animals or even would-be robbers to enter their homes. Generally, any dog door that has a Boxer on the other side of it will go untouched. In fact, because a potential thief doesn't know where your dog will be, it may serve as an even greater deterrent.

Baby gates: Another product that can facilitate house-training is the baby gate. If your dog is out of its crate, baby gates are a must for keeping it exactly where you want it, but don't count on them for total safety. The crate is the only way you will know that your Boxer is where it is supposed to be. Gates can be

Your Boxer really does want to please you, so remember to be patient, consistent, and give plenty of praise.

climbed and a determined Boxer can pull these devices from the walls. If your Boxer seems to respect the gates, great; you're one of the lucky ones. Just don't count on these products as fail-proof.

The key to successful house-training—and any form of training for that matter—is to be consistent, remain positive, and reward and praise your Boxer when it does the *right* thing. It truly wants to please you. You just have to be able to teach it what you want it to do. In the end, your patience and dedication will pay off.

Chapter Thirteen

When Good Boxers Behave Badly

No dog, not even a Boxer, is perfect all of the time. Usually, every dog possesses at least one or two habits that can drive an owner crazy unless something is done to control the situation. This chapter will cover the basic problems good Boxers sometimes display, the reasons behind these behaviors, and some solutions. With the exception of some forms of aggression, most dog behaviors can be worked through given a little perseverance, patience and creativity on the part of the owner.

Aggression

All breeds of dogs, from those bred to be ferocious guard dogs to those bred exclusively as lapdogs, have individuals within that breed that have shown varying types of aggression. Depending on the type of aggression and the way in which the situation is handled, the dog may or may not make it as a family dog.

In order to understand how to handle the different forms of aggres-

sion, it is important to recognize the characteristics of the basic types of aggression present in dogs and seek appropriate help immediately, even when these traits are present in puppies. Puppies exhibiting aggression stand probably the greatest opportunity for rehabilitation and owners should not lose this opportunity.

The following is an abbreviated guide that in no way is meant to take the place of advice and counseling from a professional trainer or animal or veterinary behaviorists. For detailed, expert information on aggression along with recommended training programs, consult *Dealing with Your Dog's Aggressive Behavior,* edited by Katherine Houpt, V.M.D., Ph.D., and Myrna E. Watanabe, Ph.D., of Cornell University College of Veterinary Medicine (Stratford, CT: Torstor Publications, 1999).

The Experts

For particularly tough problems such as aggression, it's time to call in a professional—a veterinary behaviorist. This person is to dogs as a psychiatrist is to humans. This

Boxers can be canine rototillers unless they are kept busy with more productive activities.

profession is not to be confused with an animal behaviorist. Anyone can hang out a shingle and call themselves an animal behaviorist. There are no degrees or certifications to prove an individual's abilities.

A veterinary behaviorist, however, has received extensive training above and beyond veterinary school in the field of animal behavior and is certified by the American College of Veterinary Behaviorists. Ask your veterinarian for a referral, or call the closest veterinary college and ask for a consultation. If the school is too far away, another source would be the American Veterinary Medical Association (see Useful Addresses and Literature, page 195).

If no veterinary behaviorist is within a reasonable distance, you might also consider an animal behaviorist who holds a doctorate in animal behavior and is certified by the Animal Behavior Society (see Useful Addresses and Literature, page 195). Though not able to prescribe medications or investigate possible physical disorders that could be causing some of the aggression problems, certified behaviorists can counsel owners and many times are outstanding trainers themselves.

Territorial Aggression

This form of aggression is directed toward any person or any animal that enters into what the dog considers its property. A neighbor could walk near a fence and a territorial dog will be jumping, barking, and snapping at the fence. Behaviorists say that the territorial dog's aggressive behavior is reinforced regularly because people and other dogs walk away from the fence. Dogs can become territorial of their yards, homes, even the owner's car. With laws governing dangerous dogs cropping up across the country, an owner can't afford to have a dog that thinks it's permissible to bark, snap, and even bite an "intruder," who could be the meter reader or a young child chasing after a ball.

If a dog has developed into a territorial nightmare, seek professional guidance. Discuss the situation with a trainer experienced in dealing with territorial aggression and talk to your veterinarian.

Some of the methods that may be introduced to counter the problem will involve intense owner participation. For example, no longer will your Boxer be allowed to roam the backyard unsupervised. If you have an intact male, studies have shown that neutering is effective in reducing territorial aggression in roughly 60 percent of males. Dogs that are aggressive to people who come to the door will need to learn to remain in a *down-stay* while the door is being opened.

In very serious cases of territorial aggression in which the dog does not respond to any training and in which the dog cannot be trusted with any strangers, the owner may be faced with the decision of euthanizing the dog. With so many good Boxer temperaments in this world, it's just not worth it to put anyone at risk because of an uncontrollable dog.

Dog-Dog Aggression

Rusty is good with small children and has never met a stranger. He greets the mailman with gusto, anticipating a delectable treat. Every human being is an opportunity to share a little more Boxer love. But, when another dog—any dog—

Neutering males will help curb their desire to scale fences and leave your property.

crosses Rusty's path, he turns into a snarling, growling terror. What's wrong?

Boxers that love people but can't tolerate other dogs are called "dog aggressive." This trait is not uncommon among Boxers. They wouldn't hurt a human, and would probably give their life to a total stranger, but every new dog they meet is a new challenge. Without appropriate behavioral training, Rusty could be,

however, a potentially dangerous dog to other dogs.

It is believed that most dogs wouldn't display dog-dog aggression if they were properly socialized with other dogs and weren't given up or sold before eight weeks of age. There are some dogs, however, that don't seem to be as responsive to environmental factors. Other dogs, such as adopted dogs, lack manners with other dogs because their prior owner failed them in this respect. Whatever the cause of the aggression, many trainers say there is hope to control this form of aggression. If a Boxer is displaying this type of aggression, even to a small degree, the owner should seek the advice of a trained professional to make sure this behavior is not encouraged and is either eliminated or reduced to a controllable state.

Some of the techniques that are currently being used to control aggression toward other dogs include extensive obedience training in order to assure that when you put your dog in a *down-stay* as a dog passes by, it will remain in that *down-stay.* The *down-stay* is a position in which the dog is not in a position of power, nor is it quite as able to bark or bite—if it stays in this position. In any case, do not allow your dog to approach strange dogs, and muzzle it if there is any chance it might pull away from you; just about any Boxer is capable of this if it really sets its mind to it. If you keep your Boxer in the yard by means of an invisible (buried) electric fence, consider another fence. The hidden fence will keep your Boxer in but it will not keep other dogs and animals from entering your yard, perhaps for the last time.

Note: Occasionally, a Boxer will get into a battle with another Boxer of the same sex. If it's not decided at this point which dog is dominant and which is submissive, the dogs may hold grudges against each other for life. Neutering will help to defray the friction in many dogs; however, spaying does not have the same effect with dog-aggressive females.

Aggression Toward Humans

Aggression toward people is a serious flaw and any attempts to rehabilitate an adult that shows this type of aggression should be taken with great gravity and a complete understanding of the repercussions should the dog not rehabilitate.

The types of aggression that may be displayed by a dog include fear aggression toward all people or to a certain class of people, such as children or men in uniform, dominance aggression, such as growling at the owner when given a command or correction, possessive aggression, such as growling or biting when the owner attempts to take away a chew bone or food, and predatory aggression, in which people are viewed as prey.

Fear aggression is one type of aggression that can be worked with quite successfully with some dogs, depending on the age of the dog and the extent and type of fear. Behaviorists commonly recommend a program of desensitization, in which the dog is rewarded for showing nonfearful behaviors in situations that would have previously evoked a fearful response.

Possessive aggression is another type of aggression in which trainers note a potential for substantial improvement in the dog's behaviors with appropriate training. If the item is simple, such as a chew bone, the dog is simply not allowed to have that particular item anymore. Dogs that are possessive of food can sometimes be rehabilitated too. If the possession is a bigger item, however, such as a family member, the complications of modifying the dog's behaviors become much more difficult and the chances for a total rehabilitation are much less likely.

Dominance aggression is the most difficult form of aggression to deal with and depending on how dominant the dog is with the owner, it can be extremely dangerous to the owner. Behaviorists say that though the problem may be controlled with extensive training, the owner will never be able to totally trust the dog. In dangerous cases of dominance aggression, the owner must con-sider the decision to euthanize the dog. A dog is meant to be a faithful companion, not a daily threat to the hand that feeds it, literally.

Predatory aggression is the most unpredictable and dangerous form of aggression in dogs. In this form of aggression, the dog sees people as prey. (It is a higher level of the same prey drive that makes dogs good ball chasers.) The object is not to chase the person out of the dog's territory or to exert itself as the boss, but to hunt down and kill the person. What creates a strong predatory drive in some dogs is not totally understood, but fortunately it is extremely rare—practically unheard of, in fact—in the Boxer. A common underlying thread discovered among fatal prey dog bite cases, however, was that the dog's owner was a social misfit and raised

Good manners are a learned process for the Boxer.

the dog in total isolation. Frightening indeed, but it gives the pet owner some insight as to just how important proper socialization of a dog is.

Note: It is a natural reaction for a dog to bite or snap when it is in pain. For this reason, an owner should never attempt to handle an injured or wounded Boxer without muzzling it first. A bite that is given in reaction to pain is not generally considered a form or aggression.

Other Common Behavior Problems

On a lighter note, the following behaviors are those that can be seen in many Boxers, particularly those that are left to their own devices during the day or night to keep busy. Often, the simplest solution is to give the dog a job and keep it busy. Unfortunately, because of many owners' working schedules, the simplest solution is not always the easiest. Few dog owners can spend 20 or more hours a day with their dogs unless they have a home-based business. Or, unless the dogs *are* their business.

The following are some suggestions to help owners assist their dogs in overcoming what could develop into bad habits.

Barking

Boxers are not known to be "barky" dogs; they typically sound the alert and then quickly settle down when the "all's well" sign is given by the owner. There are always exceptions to the rule, however, or those Boxers who feel it is their duty to be both day watchman and night sentry.

One solution is to bring the dog inside. Sounds simplistic, but, it works. If a dog is outside, it is bored. It is also stimulated by all sorts of sounds. If it feels a particular sound is strange, unfamiliar, or threatening, it will begin barking until the threat is gone or the noise has silenced. Of course, these heroics are not admired by your neighbors under whose window your dog is barking. With the dog inside, it is no longer stimulated by the sounds and it settles in for the night.

But, what if you have a dog door and your dog runs in and out all day for every little sound and you're at the office and can't monitor your dog's activities? This one is tougher because the dog is serving as a watchdog, which you want it to do. What you don't want is incessant barking of a dog that likes to bark just to hear its own bark.

Owners of livestock guardian dogs, which are known for their nocturnal barking, say that spray collars can be quite effective in training a dog not to bark all the time. Every time the dog barks, it is sprayed with a bad-tasting but harmless solution. Some dogs, however, figure the collar out and purposely bark until the liquid is gone so they can bark away at their leisure. Another option might be to consider using an electronic

A special collar can be used to inhibit barking; however, giving the Boxer attention and not allowing it to be alone for any length of time usually curb the boredom that causes barking problems.

stimulation collar at a very low setting. This type of collar must be used only when the owner is home and can monitor the dog's activities. Also, because the collar can deliver a jolt to such a shorthaired breed as the Boxer, great care needs to be taken not to abuse the collar.

Digging

Dogs dig for many different reasons. Sometimes digging trenches just seems like a lot of fun to a Boxer. Other days, when it is warm outside, a big hole in the ground would provide a nice cool spot to snooze. Then there are Boxers that bury their bones and are perpetually digging them back up. And there are still other Boxers that will burrow a tunnel to escape under the fence.

The answer to the bored dog is, of course, either to keep it occupied and with the owner, or confined to an area where it can't get in trouble when the owner isn't looking. The dog that is digging for a cooler place needs to be kept inside on warm days or provided a shady, breezy spot in the yard for limited time periods. Owners of dogs that enjoy digging have had some success with designating a digging patch in their yards for the dog and even burying items for their dogs to uncover. Another solution might be to install a partial underground electric fence that limits the Boxer's activities to one area of the yard, or to build a kennel run for the dog to use when the owner cannot be in the yard to supervise where and when the dog is digging.

For the Boxer that is digging its way under the fence, determine why it has such an intense desire to leave its home. If the Boxer is a male, neutering will calm the "call of the wild" and will help to keep your wayward male at home. Spaying will also help a female Boxer from attracting all the neighborhood dogs from digging under your fence, and will serve to take her drive away for meeting up with would be dog suitors.

Chewing

Mostly a problem with teething puppies, the best way to control unwanted chewing is to provide your Boxer plenty of safe chew bones and toys. If the dog still can't be trusted, or if it has a particular liking for sixteenth-century antiques, it will be necessary to keep the dog and its teeth away from anything you don't want reconfigured. This can be accomplished with judiciously crating the dog when you can't watch it, or by confining it to an area of the home in which there's nothing of value that can be destroyed.

Nipping

Sometimes puppies will jump up and nip at children's clothing, limbs, and such. This is a puppy game that must be nipped in the bud. Puppies that nip children or their owners are looking at their human family as equals, in this case, as puppies. This association must be stopped so that the dog realizes that it is on the bottom of the totem pole in the house. This is achieved by involving your children in training the dog. Very young children can sit in a parent's lap and give the dog a treat after it obeys a command given by the parent. If the nipping and rough play accelerates because your children won't listen to you and persist in screaming and running and jumping around, encouraging this rough play, then separate the children from the Boxer and vice versa. Once the puppy progresses through the teething stage, the primary time for nipping and chewing on children, you may find the situation settles down substantially. If not, continue training your Boxer and your children to respect each other, and separate children from dogs when you cannot give them your undivided attention.

Jumping Up

Boxers are enthusiastic, good-hearted dogs that love their people. And what better way to show their favorite humans just how much they love them than by jumping up and wrapping their forelegs around them? Bam! The only problem is that even a medium-weight Boxer is capable of tumbling a sturdy, unsuspecting individual.

The best way to discourage this exuberant greeting is to teach your Boxer the *sit-stay*. When introducing your dog to strangers or friends, put the dog in a *sit-stay* and require the dog to remain in this position when greeting people. With this training tip a lot fewer people will be bowled over. Of course, getting your Boxer to *sit-stay* when *you* come home may be a bit more difficult.

Jumping Over

Boxers are an athletic breed and leaping over the backyard fence may be a piece of cake for the determined Boxer. This leaping or climbing ability is a good way to wind up with a lost or stolen Boxer. To squelch the incidences of fence climbing, the owner needs to take a look at why the dog wants to get over the fence. Is the dog bored? Is it left out alone in the backyard for hours on end? (A big no, no with a Boxer.) If so, then human contact may be all this fence jumper needs to stay home.

The problem could also be that you have an intact male Boxer in search of a female in season. Neutering will solve this problem, but if the dog has already learned how to climb the fence, other steps may need to be taken to insure the safety of the dog.

Daily exercise and regular training can work wonders with your Boxer's behaviors.

Teaching your Boxer the sit-stay *command can help curb playful, but powerful, jumping up.*

First of all, is the fence high enough? It should be at least 6 feet (1.8 m) tall. Is the fence climbable? Chain-link fences can give dogs a foothold, whereas, a solid privacy fence is flat and slick. In severe cases of fence jumping, the fence may have to be constructed with a slightly inward slope. Or a hidden electric fence could be used around the base of the fence. And finally, the dog could be allowed an exercise run with a roof to prevent future escapes.

Separation Anxiety

Separation anxiety is usually experienced by a puppy when it first arrives at its new owner's home. Everything is new and strange and the puppy misses the warmth and security of its mother and littermates.

Of course, it quickly overcomes this anxiety when it realizes just how much fun it is to live with people.

There are cases, however, in which the separation anxiety continues into the dog's adulthood. Whenever the owner leaves the home, the dog goes wild with almost outright terror. Excessive panting, howling, crying, pacing, and elimination are all behaviors the Boxer might exhibit. Some cases of separation anxiety can be so severe that crating alone is not enough to prevent the dog from injuring itself, and medication is required to prevent the dog from injuring itself, according to some veterinary experts.

Some cases of separation anxiety can be calmed by determining the triggering stimuli for the behavior and providing a new consequence. In other words, if every time you open the front door, you leave, then practice opening the front door without leaving. Then when you must leave, go quietly out a side door.

A Special Case: The Deaf Dog

The deaf Boxer is not a problem dog but it does present a different training scenario. Since the deaf Boxer can't hear, you must be able to get its attention in a way other than by using your voice. This means you must cross its line of vision using an object, such as a ball or a beam of light. Deaf Boxers can also be trained to look at their owners when given a pagerlike buzz from an electronic collar or similar device.

The key is to get the dog's attention. Once this is achieved, the dog can be trained with hand signals using the same positive reward training methods as those used for hearing dogs. Treats are critical to get the dog's attention, and consistency in hand signals is also key. Many owners of deaf dogs use American Sign Language, but any form of signals that are easily seen can be used.

Owners who have trained deaf Boxers say they feel the deaf Boxer is actually in some ways more attentive than its hearing counterparts. Because the dog cannot hear, it depends on its owner for some guidance. Some deaf dog owners relate that their dogs are so focused on their hands that the dogs attempt to interpret what their owners are saying when they are actually just "talking" with their hands to a friend.

For more information on training deaf dogs, see Useful Addresses and Literature, page 196.

Chapter Fourteen

Beyond Basics: Getting Involved

Looking for something to do with your Boxer? There are at least a dozen activities you can become involved in with your dog. The Boxer is such a talented, agile breed, and is so eager and willing to work with its owner, it would be a shame *not* to become involved in a sport.

Following are summaries of both competitive and noncompetitive activities that welcome Boxers.

Competitive Activities for Boxers

In competitive events, you and your Boxer will be competing against other dog-human partners. Since there are placements—some dog must win—there is competition. In many of these sports, however, the competition is congenial and competitors support each other's efforts. Which sport you choose to participate in largely depends on your Boxer's talents and your dedication to training your dog.

Agility

Agility is the fastest-growing dog sport in the United States. It has literally taken the country by storm. Competitors relate that in many areas of the country, some of the fiercest competition is just in getting registered for an event. Sometimes the only way to assure registration in an event is to overnight-mail the entry so it arrives on the opening day for registration.

There is a reason for the booming popularity of this sport. It's fun. Training schools, which are popping up all over the country, relate that most people begin agility classes just to have fun with their dogs. Pretty soon, they're hooked, and off they go into the world of competition.

Agility is modeled after the equine open jumping classes in which horse and rider are required to complete a course of obstacles in the fastest time with the fewest number of faults. In this case, faults are refusals to jump, poles that are knocked down, a foot in the water jump, and so on. In agility, the dog must navi-

The Boxer's great athleticism makes it a natural for many sports, including Agility.

gate through a series of obstacles, too. Under the direction of its owner, the Boxer must jump over hurdles, weave through poles, slide through tunnels, and trot over a teeter-totter. The dog with the fastest time through the course with the fewest faults is the winner.

In order to compete in agility, the Boxer must be physically mature (older than at least one year), fit, and have no orthopedic problems, such as elbow or hip dysplasia. It should also know the basic commands: *sit, down, stay, come.* Dogs of all athletic ability will have fun in this event; the truly agile and keen dogs will excel. Trainers say that even shy dogs do well in this sport, and that it is thought that working in agility with a fearful dog produces a much more confident companion.

Organizations that sanction agility competitions can be found by contacting the American Kennel Club (see Useful Addresses and Literature, page 00).

To find an agility training club, ask your local obedience club for referrals. If the local club doesn't have agility courses, they will know who in the area does.

Conformation

Dog showing is truly a favorite hobby among dog fanciers. Dogs are judged against each other in order to find a Winners Dog and Winners Bitch. Points toward a conformation championship are awarded for the top male or top female in the breed at the show on a given day. Obviously, with the numbers of Boxers being shown today, it is very difficult to win and it takes a very well-put-together Boxer to win in the show ring.

Once winners are found from the nonchampion males and females, the winning dogs are then shown against the specials. The specials are dogs that have already achieved their championships. From this class,

a Best of Breed and Best of Opposite Sex are chosen. Though this moment is extremely exciting, it isn't over yet. The BOB from the Boxer class then goes on to compete against BOBs from all other breeds from the working group. Including the Boxer, the working group is composed of 21 breeds, including Rottweilers, Doberman Pinschers, Great Danes, and Samoyeds.

When a group winner has been selected, it then waits for the final class: Best in Show. Here the winners from sporting, hound, working, terrier, toy, nonsporting, and herding

The conformation ring is keenly competitive and the decision as to which dog is the best in a class is subjective, and to some extent, varies from judge to judge.

groups compete for the ultimate award, a BIS (Best in Show).

It takes more than owning a drop-dead gorgeous Boxer to win in the breed ring; it also takes a dog with a tremendous temperament and movement. And the handler must know how to show off his or her dog to its best advantage. Because of the breed's popularity and the immense sizes of some classes, a person can own a great dog and be a skilled handler but find it difficult to "finish" a dog's championship. Often, in these cases, an owner will consider hiring a professional handler to show a Boxer.

If you decide to show your dog yourself, there are usually classes that you can take at a local obedience club in show handling. These people will give you the tips and instruction you will need to present your Boxer. If you truly have a magnificent dog, you will be able to succeed in the show ring. It may take a little longer if you do it yourself and it won't be inexpensive traveling to all those shows, but the final rewards will be all yours and your Boxer's.

For more information on upcoming shows, contact the American Kennel Club.

Flyball

This sport must have been designed with Boxers in mind. It involves running, jumping over hurdles, catching tennis balls, and getting a little wild. If you have an energetic Boxer that has quick speed and is adept at catching tennis balls, you might really enjoy this sport.

Flyball consists of teams of four dogs and their handlers. It's a relay race in which the fastest team wins. The first dog is sent out to retrieve the flyball. It jumps over a series of hurdles, reaches the box in which the balls are contained, and steps on the trigger that releases the balls. The ball pops up in the air, the dog catches it, and races back to the team where the next dog and handler are ready to go.

To compete in flyball, your Boxer must be healthy and must enjoy being around other dogs. The competitions get noisy and both fans and participants are very keyed up. The sanctioning organization is the North American Flyball Association (NAFA), which also publishes a list of upcoming events. NAFA also maintains a list of teams. If there is no flyball club in your area, NAFA can help you find equipment to develop your own team. The NAFA can be reached by writing: North American Flyball Association, 1002 E. Samuel Avenue, Peoria Heights, Illinois 61614.

Musical Canine Freestyle

Modeled after an equine dressage class that requires riders to perform dressage movements with their horses in sync with music, musical canine freestyle is a relatively new sport that began as a demonstration in Canada. Musical canine freestyle involves complex, rapid maneuvers by the dog and handler choreographed to

Before you embark on a demanding sport with your Boxer, it should be at least one year old and should have received a clean bill of health from its veterinarian.

music. Owners and dogs are often in costume.

Classes include on lead, off lead, single dog and handler, and multi-dog and handler. If you ever get a chance to see this class, do it. Musical canine freestyle is always a showstopper and pulls the largest audience of all at shows. To become adept at the sport takes a lot of work, according to handlers, and an enthusiastic dog. Because of the Boxer's agility, intelligence, and great physique, it has the potential to be a top performer in this sport. Of course, the owner must be willing to be seen in public, dancing with his or her dog!

For the names and addresses of canine Freestyle organizations, see Useful Addresses and Literature, page 196.

Obedience

Your Boxer doesn't need to have picture-perfect conformation to

The basic level of obedience requires that the dog heel sharply in a figure eight pattern around two people, as shown here.

become an Obedience champion; it just needs to have an eagerness to learn, a willingness to please, and an owner who can accept the challenges of training such an intelligent dog. The American Kennel Club offers five titles in obedience competitions: Companion Dog (CD), Companion Dog Excellent (CDX), Utility Dog (UD), and Utility Dog Excellent (UDX). The Obedience Trial Championship (OTCh) title is awarded to dogs that have earned a UD and have earned 100 points. Points are tallied according to dogs defeated in classes, placement, and so on. There is also a National Obedience Championship competition that is run once a year by the National Obedience Association.

The AKC also offers "nonregular" classes in obedience, such as the brace class in which two dogs of the same breed are shown unattached or coupled, veterans' class for dogs aged seven or older, and the team class made up of teams of four dogs and handlers.

In the regular classes, each title requires three passing scores or "legs" to achieve that level's title. To be awarded a CD, for example, a Boxer must receive a passing score in three separate trials. Exercises that are required for the entry level obedience class (CD) are:
• heel on leash and figure eight
• stand for examination
• heel free
• recall
• long *sit*
• long *down*.

To receive a qualifying score in the Open class (CDX), the Boxer must successfully complete the following exercises:
• heel free and figure eight
• drop on recall
• retrieve on flat
• retrieve over high jump
• broad jump
• long *sit*
• long *down.*

Utility requirements are a step harder from the Open class:
• signal exercise
• scent discrimination (article 1)
• scent discrimination (article 2)
• directed retrieve
• moving stand and examination
• directed jumping

To excel in obedience, it is wise to hook up with a good obedience club early on in your training (see Finding a Good Training Center, page 159). A positive attitude is a must to keep your Boxer enthusiastic about its training!

For more information on obedience trials and the AKC's regulations, contact the American Kennel Club.

Schutzhund

Schutzhund is not a dangerous sport for dangerous dogs. Quite to the contrary, a Boxer will do well in this sport only if it is extremely intelligent and possesses great mental soundness. Aggressive, flighty, or unstable dogs will not be able to pass even the most basic level of these tests.

Schutzhund is not all protection work, as some people may think. It is really a test of the versatility of the working dog. In other words, the protection test is only a part of the entire Schutzhund test. In fact, before a dog can even be tested at the first level of Schutzhund work, which includes tracking and obedience as well as protection work, the dog must pass an obedience test and earn its companion dog title (BH).

Schutzhund titles that can be earned include BH (companion dog), Sch.A, Sch.I, Sch.II, Sch.III. It is important when training for Schutzhund work to find a good working club that has experience with Boxers, if possible. The United States Boxer Association is a national club developed to meet the needs of the working Boxer. The association and its members are very helpful in directing Boxer owners to training information. The association also holds its own Schutzhund trials on an annual basis. For information, contact the United States Boxer Association (see Useful Addresses and Literature, page 195).

Tracking

Boxers are noted for their scenting abilities. Historically, they have been used as tracking dogs and more recently as drug dogs that must locate illegal drugs. In other words, even if your Boxer comes from generations of show dogs and hasn't been asked to track anything, odds are that your dog will still perform well in this sport.

The American Kennel Club offers three levels of tracking: Tracking

Schutzhund work includes protection training in addition to obedience skills and tracking.

Dog (TD), Tracking Dog Excellent (TDX), and Variable Surface Training (VST). A Boxer that achieves all three titles is awarded a tracking championship. The tests are pass/fail and are not competitive.

The TD requires a dog to track a fresh scent through turns to find a scented article. The TDX level takes the dog and handler through a more difficult course of varied, and many times physically challenging, terrain.

The scent is older, the trail is longer, and there are physical obstacles, such as water and fallen logs. The final test offered by the AKC is the VST, which was designed to simulate a realistic tracking of a person. The test requires that the dog track a scent over both vegetative and man-made surfaces.

To find a tracking club, your first call should be to the local obedience club. Many times these clubs have a subset of members that are actively involved in tracking. For more information on tracking, contact the American Kennel Club.

Noncompetitive Activities for Boxers

In addition to the competitive activities sponsored by a variety of organizations, there are several noncompetitive activities that are well suited for the Boxer.

Backpacking

If you are an outdoors person and are thinking of taking your Boxer along with you on day hikes and perhaps even an overnight trip, you can.

A well-fitted pack and conditioning are essential to successful backpacking with your Boxer.

As long as your Boxer is not suffering from any health problems and is in good shape, it can be conditioned to carry a backpack with much of its own supplies. There are now companies that manufacture backpacks specifically designed for dogs, so a comfortable fit is possible.

Conditioning your Boxer to its pack is necessary and should be done gradually. Dogs in good shape can generally carry 10 to 15 percent of their body weight in the pack. Exceptionally muscular Boxers may be able to carry as much as 25 percent, but don't push it. Precautions to take when hiking with your Boxer include applying a topical dose of flea and tick preventive prior to your trip, keeping the Boxer on a leash (retractable or recall leashes allow your Boxer to explore safely), and keeping an eye on the temperature. As noted, Boxers do not do well in warm or cold weather, so your best hiking seasons will most likely be spring and fall.

Canine Good Citizen

Do you want to prove that your Boxer is a model canine citizen but you aren't interested in the competitive nature of obedience trials? You may be interested in the AKC's Canine Good Citizen (CGC) Program. The CGC was developed by the AKC to encourage dog owners to teach their canines good manners, both in the home and in public. Many therapy organizations require their dog-human partners to pass the test as a prerequisite to therapy work.

The CGC is a pass/fail test that examines the dog and owner at several levels. To achieve CGC certification, the dog must be presented as a well-groomed dog. It must be willing to approach a stranger and sit quietly as the stranger pets the dog. The dog must show that it can walk nicely on a leash, walk through a crowd of people on a loose leash, and perform the basic commands, *sit, down, stay,* and *come.* The dog also must be able to behave well around other dogs.

For more information on the CGC program or for a complete set of test rules, an information kit, and a schedule of testing locations and dates, contact the American Kennel Club, Canine Good Citizen Program.

Carting/Drafting/Driving

The Boxer can pull its weight. If your Boxer is healthy and in good condition, you may enjoy teaching it to pull a small cart. (The famous Friederun von Miram-Stockmann is pictured in an historic photo in which she is driving a small carriage that is being pulled by four of her Boxers.)

The terms carting, drafting, and driving have similar meanings when it comes to dog power and all can be performed by Boxers. Carting involves pulling a wheeled vehicle with or without a rider. Drafting is pulling with no passenger, but perhaps a small load. Driving involves the dog pulling a cart and following the commands of the driver of the cart.

Additional terms of the sport include a cart, which is a two-wheeled vehicle, a wagon, which has four wheels, and a travois, which has no wheels and is a sort of sled that is used to drag loads containing various items. The two-wheeled cart is the lightest and easiest vehicle to maneuver and is perhaps most suited to the Boxer, which is much smaller in size than many breeds that participate in this sport.

Necessary equipment will include a harness that is comfortable and fits your dog well. You will also need a cart; there are companies that specialize in carting equipment for dogs. Experienced carters recommend waiting until your Boxer is fully developed and mature, which would mean no pulling before the age of 18 months, perhaps even two years.

For more information on carting, the following books and videos are available: *An Introduction to Canine Carting with Beth Ostrander* is a 60-minute video illustrating basic carting, use of the equipment, and training techniques (available through *Dog Works* at http://www.dogworks.com/books/bkdraft.htm); *Newfoundland Draft Work* by Consie Powell (also available through *Dog Works*); and *Draft Equipment Guide* by Roger Powell also available through *Dog Works*).

Community Service Activities

Pet therapy: There are many benefits of dog ownership. According to various studies, dog owners tend to be happier, healthier, and live longer. Why not share some of the Boxer love with a person who is less fortunate than you? If you have a Boxer that is well trained and is not easily rattled by an accidental ear pulling, it may have what it takes to become a therapy dog or a pet visitor.

Therapy dogs are canines that are incorporated into a health care facility's care plans. In other words, the visits made by the dogs and handlers are part of the patient's therapy program and are used to make specific gains in the patient's progress. With pet visitation, the dog's visits are made to brighten up the spirits of the facility's residents, as well as add some spontaneity to the schedules of the staff. Both forms of therapy are equally rewarding, and the difference in them can be a matter of how the facility approaches and incorporates the visits into its overall programing.

For a dog to become a therapy dog, it generally must possess its Canine Good Citizen certification (see page 192), and be certified by a recognized animal assisted therapy (AAT) association. Certification by the AAT association often requires a temperament test and the completion of and graduation from an AAT program.

One AAT organization is the Delta Society (see Useful Addresses and Literature for contact information). This organization provides home study kits, as well as a plethora of information brochures, pamphlets, articles and other materials. Another organization is Therapy Dogs International, Inc.

Search and rescue: Though limited in hot or extremely cold weather, the Boxer can be trained for search and rescue (SAR) work. This work involves tracking over both old and new trails in real-life situations. Though SAR volunteers relate that in some areas of the country the majority of searches are for Alzheimer patients who have wandered off, other searches include lost children, missing adults, and the recovery of a deceased individual. Though civilian SAR volunteers are used only in non-violent situations—murder searches are performed by law enforcement agents—the work can become dangerous. It has been known to happen that a lost person turned out to be murdered, with the murderer still close by.

SAR is virtually a full-time, unpaid volunteer job. Members of local SAR teams must be available to leave at a moment's notice and travel, sometimes to distant or even international locations. Once in the field, the dog-human team must be able to survive in the wilderness on its own for 24 hours. Training is also rigorous for both dog and owner, but SAR volunteers would have it no other way.

This activity is certainly exciting and will tax both your dog's and your physical and mental stamina. It is also a deeply rewarding activity. To find an SAR team in your area, volunteers suggest contacting your local law enforcement agency to find out with whom they work. Other people who might know who to contact would include members of your local obedience club. SAR units affiliated with the American Rescue Dog Association (ARDA) can be located by accessing the association's web page or writing to the association (see Useful Addresses and Literature for contact information).

Useful Addresses and Literature

Organizations
Breed Information
American Boxer Club

The current secretary of the breed club can be contacted for breed information. Call the AKC and ask for the current address of the ABC's secretary. Internet savvy fanciers can locate much information at the club's web site: *http://www.akc.org/clubs/abc.*

German Boxer Klub
Boxer-Klub E.V. Sitz München
Veldener Str 64+66
81241 Munich, Germany
011 49-89-54670812
web site: http://www.bk-muenchen.
    de/english.htm.

United States Boxer Association
W3595 Larson Road
Mindoro, Wisconsin 54644
web site: http://members.aol.com/
    Usabox

American Kennel Club
5580 Centerview Drive, Suite 200
Raleigh, North Carolina 27606-3390
(919) 233-3600
web site: www.akc.org

United Kennel Club
100 E. Kilgore Road
Kalamazoo, Michigan 49001-5598

Agility
North American Dog Agility Council
HCR2
Box 277
St. Marie, Idaho 83861

United States Dog Agility
    Association
P.O. Box 850955
Richardson, Texas 75085
(214) 231-9700

Behavior
Animal Behavior Society
2611 East 10th Street, Office 170
Indiana University
Bloomington, Indiana 47408-2603
(812) 856-5541
Web site: www.animalbehavior.org/
    ABS
E-mail: aboffice@indiana.edu

American Veterinary Medical
    Association
1931 N. Meacham Road
    Suite 100
Schaumburg, Illinois 60173-4360
(847) 925-8070

Boxer Rescue
American Boxer Rescue Association
Tracy Hendrickson
4412 W. Kent Circle
Broken Arrow, Oklahoma 74014
(918) 665-1765
Web site: www.jps.net/Boxer4me

Search and Rescue
American Rescue Dog Association
P.O. Box 151
Chester, New York 10918
Web site: www.ardainc.org

Deaf Dogs
Deaf Dog Education Action Fund
P.O. Box 369
Boonville, California 95415
Web sites: www.deafdogs.org
Ddeaf@aol.com

Freestyle
Canine Freestyle Federation
Joan Tennille
4207 Minton Drive
Fairfax, Virginia 22032

Musical Canine Sports International, Inc.
Sharon Tutt
16665 Parkview Place
Surrey, British Columbia V4N 1YB
Canada
(604) 581-3641

Schutzhund
United Schutzhund Clubs of
    America
3810 Paule Avenue
St. Louis, Missouri 63125
(314) 638-9686

Therapy Dogs
The Delta Society
289 Perimeter Road East
Renton, Washington 98055-1329
1-800-869-6898
Web site: www.deltasociety.com

Therapy Dogs International, Inc.
88 Bartley Road
Flanders, New Jersey 07836
(973) 252-9800
Web site: www.tdi_dog.org

Books
Activities

Agility: Simmons-Moeke, Jane. *Agility Training: The Fun Sport for All Dogs.* New York: Howell Book House, 1992.

Backpacking: LaBelle, Charlene. *A Guide to Backpacking with Your Dog.* Loveland, CO: Alpine Publications, 1992.

Canine Good Citizen: Volhard, Joachim. *The Canine Good Citizen: Every Dog Can Be One.* New York; Howell Book House, 1997.

Conformation: Coile, Caroline D. *Show Me! A Dog Show Primer.* Hauppauge, NY: Barron's Educational Series, 1997.

Hall, Lynn. *Dog Showing for Beginners.* New York: Howell Book House, 1994.

Deaf Dogs: Eaton, Barry. *Hear, Hear! A Guide to Training a Deaf Puppy,* 2nd edition. Hampshire, England: Holmes & Sons, 1998.

Sternberg, Martin L.A. *American Sign Language Dictionary.* New York, Harper Reference, 1998.

Flyball: Olson, Lonnie. *Flyball Racing: The Dog Sport for Everyone.* New York: Macmillan General Reference, 1997.

Schutzhund: Barwig, Susan. *Schutzhund: Theory and Training Methods.* New York: Howell Book House, 1991.

Search & Rescue: American Dog Rescue Association. *Search and Rescue Dogs: Training Methods.* New York: Howell Book House, 1991.

Therapy: Davis, Kathy Diamond. *Therapy Dogs: Training Your Dog to Reach Others.* New York: Howell Book House, 1992.

Tracking: Brown, Tom. *The Science and Art of Tracking.* New York: Penguin USA, 1999.

Adult Dog Adoption

Benjamin, Carol Lea. *Second Hand Dog: How to Turn Yours Into a First Rate Pet.* Forest City, CA: IDG Books Worldwide, 1994.

Hustace Walker, Joan. *Dog Adoption.* Indianapolis: ICS, 1997.

Palika, Liz. *Save That Dog: Everything You Need to Know About Adopting a Purebred Rescue Dog.* Forest City, CA: IDG Books Worldwide, 1997.

Papurt, Myrna L. *Saved: A Guide to Success with Your Shelter Dog.* Hauppauge, NY: Barron's Educational Series, 1997.

General

Hutchings, Tim. *The Complete Boxer.* New York: Howell Book House, 1998.

McFadden, Billie. *The New Boxer.* New York: Howell Book House, 1989.

Tomita, Richard. *The World of the Boxer.* Neptune City, NJ: TFH Publications, 1998.

Grooming, Care and Nutrition

Ackerman, Lowell. *Dr. Ackerman's Book of Boxers* Neptune City, New Jersey: TFH, 1996.

———. *Owner's Guide to Dog Health.* DVM Neptune City, NJ: TFH, 1995.

Cusick, William D. and Luana Luther. *Canine Nutrition: Choosing the Best Food for Your Breed.* Wilsonville, OR: Doral Publishing, Inc., 1997.

Foster, Race and Marty Smith, *What's the Diagnosis? Understanding Your Dog's Health Problems.* New York: Howell Book House, 1995.

Pinney, Chris C. *Caring for Your Older Dog.* Hauppauge, NY: Barron's Educational Series, 1995.

History

Grosse, Joachim and Peter Holzhausen. *Unser Hund Ein Boxer.* Munich, Germany: Boxer-Klub E.V. Sitz München, 1994.

Thurston, Mary Elizabeth. *The Lost History of the Canine Race.* Kansas City, MO: Andrews and McMeel, 1996.

Puppy Ownership

Bailey, Gwen. *The Perfect Puppy: How to Raise a Well-behaved Dog.* New York: Readers Digest, 1996.

Palika, Liz. *The Complete Idiot's Guide to Raising a Puppy.* New York: Howell Book House, 1998.

Ross, John and Barbara McKinney. *Puppy Preschool: Raising Your*

Puppy Right–Right from the Start! New York: St. Martins Press, 1996.

Training/Behavior

Dunbar, Ian. *Dog Behavior: An Owner's Guide to a Happy Healthy Pet.* Forest City, CA: IDG Books Worldwide, 1998.

———. *How to Teach a New Dog Old Tricks.* Berkeley, CA: James and Kenneth Publishing, 1998.

Pryor, Karen. *Don't Shoot the Dog* (2nd edition). North Bend, WA: Sunshine Books, 1999.

Siegal, Mordecai and Matthew Margolis. *Good Dog, Bad Dog: Dog Training Made Easy.* New York: Henry Holt & Company, 1991.

Videos

Sirius Puppy Training Video by Ian Dunbar (Berkeley, CA: James & Kenneth Publishers, 1998), 90-minute VHS.

The Click and Treat Kit (video and booklet) by Gary Wilkes (Mesa, AZ: Click and Treat™ Products); Web site: www.clickandtreat.com.

Training the Companion Dog, Volumes I–IV, by Ian Dunbar (Berkeley, CA: James & Kenneth Publishers, 1998), 60-minute VHS (each volume)

Woof! It's a Dog's Life by Matthew Margolis (PBS, 1998), 4-tape series, 60-minutes each VHS.

Magazines and Web Sites

Boxer Review
8760 Applan Way
Los Angeles, California 90046
(323) 654-3147

Boxer Underground (A bi-monthly Internet magazine)
Web site:
www.boxerunderground.com

Boxer World (informative web site)
www.boxerworld.com

Deaf Dogs (web site)
www.kiva.net/~lindsay/deafdogs

Deaf Dog Mailing List (free listing)
E-mail: deaf-dogs-request@ cybervision.kwic.net
Type "subscribe deaf dogs" in the subject of your e-mail and type your name and address in the text of your e-mail.

Index